Chess Opening Traps for Kids

Graham Burgess

STEALING THE CHEESE

First published in the UK by Gambit Publications Ltd 2018
Copyright © Graham Burgess 2018
Reprinted 2023

ISBN-13: 978-1-911465-27-0
ISBN-10: 1-911465-27-9

DISTRIBUTION:

Worldwide (except USA): Central Books Ltd, 50 Freshwater Road, Chadwell Heath, London RM8 1RX, England.
Tel +44 (0)20 8986 4854 Fax +44 (0)20 8533 5821. E-mail: orders@Centralbooks.com

Gambit Publications Ltd, 27 Queens Pine, Bracknell, Berks, RG12 0TL, England.
E-mail: info@gambitbooks.com
Website (regularly updated): www.gambitbooks.com

Edited by Graham Burgess
Typeset by Petra Nunn
All illustrations by Shane Mercer
Printed and bound by TJ Books, Padstow, Cornwall, England

10 9 8 7 6 5 4 3 2

PARALYSING PINS

Gambit Publications Ltd
Directors: Dr John Nunn GM,
Murray Chandler GM, and Graham Burgess FM
German Editor: Petra Nunn WFM

Contents

RAMPANT PAWNS

Introduction

So, it's the start of a new game. The same 64 squares and the same 32 pieces. You know what you should be doing over the next few moves: control the centre, develop your pieces, keep your king safe... But why is it so difficult? Why do things go horribly wrong sometimes? Why do you finish your development and then find your pieces are badly placed?

It's because of the person sitting opposite you. *Your opponent.* Trying to do the same things you are – maybe. Not always following the 'rules' of development. Suddenly using tactics to stop you playing the moves you wanted to play. Playing odd-looking moves that you can't see how to 'punish'.

These are the ingredients missing from many opening guides. Opening play is full of tactics and tricks. Stopping the opponent's ideas is just as important as carrying out your own plans. Development means giving all your pieces something useful to do – not just moving them off their starting squares. The battle starts from move one, and you need to be fighting hard for every important square.

In this book, we'll see how **opening tactics** are used by masters to get the better of their opponents in the opening. Our traps here aren't 'bad moves that give the opponent a chance to go wrong'. That's just bad chess. No, we're looking for **good moves that give the opponent a chance to go wrong**! If we can make a whole series of good moves that cleverly prevent the opponent from playing his most useful moves, we can look forward to a great middlegame, where our pieces are working together wonderfully. And of course, if the opponent has taken one of those chances to go wrong, there might not even be a middlegame...

First things first. I am assuming you know how to play chess and you have a basic knowledge of tactics. Perhaps you have read *How to Beat Your Dad at Chess* and *Chess Tactics for Kids*. I am *not* assuming you know much about openings. If you know the names of some of the main ones, like the Sicilian and the Ruy Lopez, then that is useful, but not essential. This is a less advanced book than *Chess Openings for Kids* (which I co-authored with John Watson) and covers different aspects of opening play.

I believe the best way to learn good opening play is by example, rather than learning a set of rules to follow. If you look at modern games by masters and grandmasters, you'll find that many of their moves don't follow the opening principles you'll find in many beginners' books. *They play whatever works.* So I shall be giving just a few guiding principles, and providing many examples of good opening play. Most of the examples in this book feature quality play – up until the point where someone falls into a trap, at least!

ELASTIC
BANDS

Chess Notation

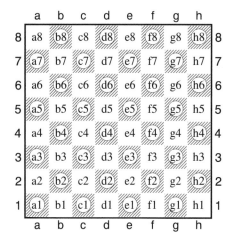

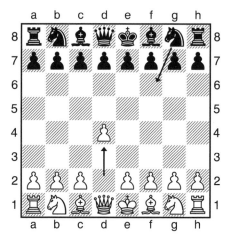

The chess moves in this book are written in the standard chess *notation* that is in use throughout the world. It can be learned by anyone in just a few minutes.

As you can see from the left-hand chessboard above, the files are labelled a-h and the ranks are numbered 1-8. This gives each square its own unique name. The pieces are shown as follows:

Knight = ♘
Bishop = ♗
Rook = ♖
Queen = ♕
King = ♔

Pawns are not given a symbol. When they move, only the *destination square* is given.

In the right-hand diagram above, White has already played the move **1 d4**. The **1** indicates the move-number, and **d4** the destination square of the white pawn. Black is about to reply **1...♘f6** (moving his knight to the **f6-square** on his *first move*).

To check you've got the hang of it, play through the following moves on your chessboard: 1 e4 c6 2 ♘f3 d5 3 ♘c3 dxe4 (the pawn on the d-file captures on e4) 4 ♘xe4 ♘d7 5 ♕e2 ♘gf6 (the knight on the g-file moves to f6 – this is a bad move!) 6 ♘d6#. Checkmate! You should now have the position shown in the first diagram on page 14.

The following additional symbols are also used:

Check	=	+
Double check	=	++
Capture	=	x
Checkmate	=	#
Castles kingside	=	0-0
Castles queenside	=	0-0-0
Good move	=	!
Bad move	=	?
Interesting idea	=	!?
Not recommended	=	?!
Brilliant move	=	!!
Disastrous move	=	??

Understanding Opening Tactics

You've probably seen a list of opening tasks, maybe something like this:

1. Put a pawn or two in the centre.
2. Move the minor pieces: knights before bishops!
3. Castle.
4. Move the queen to connect the rooks.

And then presumably you are ready to play the middlegame. As well as the dos, you are normally given a number of don'ts, such as:

1. Don't move the same piece twice.
2. Don't move the queen out early on.
3. Don't put knights on the edge.
4. Don't make lots of pawn moves.

These pieces of advice make sense in many cases, but *following them as if they are unbreakable rules will lead to bad opening play.* The traps in this book sometimes punish players who have broken them. But we also see players who have obeyed them getting into deep trouble. And the winners of the games in this book have often not followed them.

Why is this? Because **tactics** come into play! It matters if pieces are working together well. A player developing thoughtfully will beat one who is just moving his pieces out.

A couple of pages ago, I promised some general guidelines, so here goes:

1) **Play what works!** This does not mean 'play whatever you feel like', but if you are certain a move is strong, then you should play it. Check it very carefully if it seems to violate a bunch of principles and you can't believe your opponent could have allowed it.

2) **Control the centre with your pieces.** The central squares (d4, e4, d5 and e5) are really important. If your opponent can use these squares freely, you don't have a good position.

3) **Develop your pieces.** This means 'get each piece doing something useful'. It does not mean just moving them off their starting squares. Get them working together well, and you should have a choice of plans when the middlegame starts.

4) **Keep your king safe.** Always be looking for threats to your king. If it is safe where it is, then there is no rush to castle. Castle when there is a good reason to. Base your choice between kingside or queenside on how it helps your plans.

5) **Play flexibly.** If your pieces have more options, they will be ready to attack the opponent in more ways.

6) **Prevent the opponent from doing all of the above.** Obvious but often forgotten, this is a key aim of opening play.

Opening? Traps?

These words are in the title of the book, so let's be clear on what they mean!

A MOUSETRAP FOR ROOKS

The **opening** is the stage of the game where both sides are developing their pieces. For the purpose of this book, I'll extend it one move further. That is, if a player's final developing move falls into a deadly trap, I'll call this an opening trap. After all, he did not get out of the opening alive!

A **trap** is a chance for the opponent to go badly wrong. It does not need to be a move that we make with the aim of trapping the opponent. It might simply be a good move where the obvious answer just happens to lose.

Enough talk. Let's see a powerful opening trap in action.

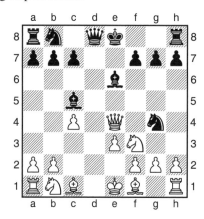

In this game, Black has played a 'gambit' – he *sacrificed* a pawn to get fast *development*.

OVERSHOT BISHOP
PERILS

White has spent a lot of time with his queen to hold on to his extra pawn. But a pawn is a pawn, and Black needs to make something dramatic happen soon. He played **8...♛d1+! 9 ♔xd1 ♞xf2+ 10 ♔c2 ♞xe4**. This is a *Geometrical Decoy* idea – we study it in Trap 71 in this book. Black's queen sacrifice set up a *knight fork* that won back the queen and a pawn. Black now has a great position.

This trick was played by a former clubmate of mine on his debut in the British championship. This was a game against a strong opponent that everyone expected him to lose! He was as surprised as anyone that he landed such a huge blow right in the opening in a big event, and, with his nerves calmed, he went on to have a great result.

Patterns

We have just seen a tactical 'pattern' in use. What do we mean by this? It is the 'skeleton' of an idea that can be used in other positions that are *similar but not identical*. In the previous diagram, plenty of the pieces could have been on different squares (e.g. pawn on h3 instead of h2) and the queen sacrifice on d1 and knight fork on f2 would still have worked. But a small change could also have ruled the idea out. Put the knight on c3 instead of b1. Or the bishop on e2 instead of f1. Either way, 8...♛d1+ would just have thrown the queen away.

So how can we work out if a pattern works in a similar position? Or a very different position? Look at:

• 'Relevant' pieces – ones that are able to interfere with the tactic or distract attention completely.
• Look at your **king** most of all.

Here is a simplified example of another of our tactical themes:

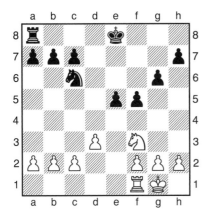

White can win a pawn with a *Pin on the e-File* (Trap 33 in this book): **1 ♘xe5! ♘xe5 2 ♖e1** followed by ♖xe5. That's nice and simple. But look what happens if we change the position of one white pawn, as follows:

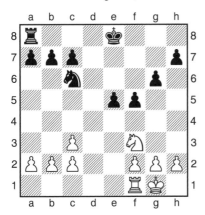

CASTLE THE
INTRUDER AWAY

Should this matter? Is this pawn *relevant*? If we **look at the kings**, we see that it is. **1 ♘xe5?? ♘xe5 2 ♖e1** is now losing for White: **2...0-0-0! 3 ♖xe5 ♖d1+** and mate next move. The *open d-file* made all the difference.

A further small change in the position – putting the white king on c1 instead of g1 – makes the trick work again:

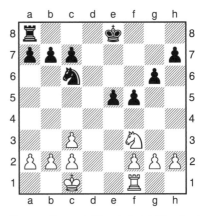

1 ♘xe5! ♘xe5 2 ♖e1 0-0-0 3 ♖xe5 wins a pawn because Black doesn't threaten to bring the rook to d1.

You might like to work out for yourself what happens with some other small modifications. For instance, what if the black pawn is on f7 instead of f5?

Of course, in an **opening trap** we have more pieces on the board than we did here. This may be confusing for players who have learned tactical patterns from a book that gave them only in simplified form. However, it is good training for 'real chess', where there will always be plenty of other pieces on the board. You will need to identify which pieces can take part in the tactic, which ones are irrelevant, and which might be able to cause trouble. Then you'll calculate to check if the tactic actually works.

Learning patterns gains *knowledge*.
Applying patterns is a *skill*.

Masters are able to use patterns they have learned in all sorts of positions that look totally different. For instance, they might use a familiar idea in a different part of the board, or with different pieces playing the key roles. Starting from a just few pieces of knowledge, we can trick and trap our opponents in many ways, in all stages of the game and in all parts of the board, whatever pieces are on it. This type of understanding takes time to develop, so let it happen gradually. After a while, you'll just start 'seeing' ideas without realizing exactly where they came from.

If you've studied a good basic tactics book, you have already seen all the tactical themes you're likely to need: pin, fork, skewer, etc. The task now is to learn how to use them, when they work, how to calculate them, use them together (*combine* them), and how to detect them. For as long as you play chess, you'll be developing these skills.

Material Values

We often have to count material to decide whether to play a move. I am sure you have seen a table of material values. Would you believe that modern chess computers use a different table?

	traditional	modern
♙	1	1
♘	3	3½
♗	3	3½
♖	5	5¼
♕	9	10

Yes, those fractions make the mental arithmetic harder! (I've even simplified a bit: the bishop is worth a little more than the knight.) But your decisions might be better using the modern values. ♕ *is* worth less than 2♗+♘. ♗+2♙ *are* worth more than ♖. But remember the standard advice: it all depends on the position. What matters most is what your pieces can do, rather than their value 'on paper'.

The modern scheme also puts a value on *time*: one move is worth about ¼ pawn. That is, if you spend two moves doing something you could have done in one move, it is like throwing away a quarter of a pawn! Something to think about!

Why should we believe any of this? Well, if those powerful computer programs use different values, they play less well against other computers. These values are the result of a lot of testing.

Don't Play for Traps with Bad Moves

After **1 e4 e5 2 ♘f3 ♘c6 3 ♗c4, 3...♘d4?** is a bad move that sets a trap. It is sometimes called the 'OMG Trap', and it has claimed countless hundreds of victims.

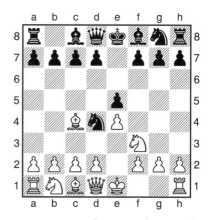

The point is **4 ♘xe5?? ♕g5! 5 ♘xf7? ♕xg2 6 ♖f1 ♕xe4+ 7 ♗e2 ♘f3#**.

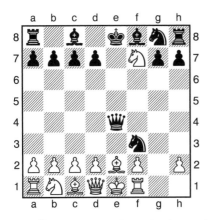

But 4 ♘xd4 and 4 0-0 are both good for White. Black has *lost time* – almost two moves in fact, or nearly half a pawn's worth if you believe the figures I gave earlier.

Still, I am sure that even after reading that, some readers will be tempted to try the move 3...♘d4?. After all, if White falls into the trap, Black wins quickly. And if he plays one of the good moves, Black is merely worse.

This is not the way to play good chess. Your opponents are not flipping a coin to choose their moves. Chess is not a horse race where it makes sense to bet on a weak

GREAT QUEEN TRAPS OF OUR TIME

option if the reward for it beating the odds is high enough. *Always choose your move assuming the opponent will make the best reply.*

Chess Opening *Blunders* for Kids?

True, this would have been a very bad title for this book! But it is also appropriate, because every time we spring a trap, it means the opponent has made a serious mistake. So when studying this book, don't focus just on the tactics, but also on the errors that allowed them. Think about whether you might have made these mistakes. Are there signs you could have spotted that would have helped you avoid them? Blunders fall into two categories:

1. The opponent makes a threat, but we don't see it.

2. The opponent has no major threat, but we play a move that allows a very strong reply. That is, we create a problem for ourselves that the opponent then pounces on.

In this book, we see case '2' a lot. Players tend to check for the opponent's threats in a position, but are less careful when looking for tactical drawbacks to the move they are about to play. So there are two things to note:

1. Before making your move, check what new possibilities it gives the opponent.

2. A cunning way to lay a trap is to think about what move the opponent wants to play next. Can you find a sly move that prepares a strong reply to that move?

This is an advanced idea, but very important in chess, and a skill you will need to develop in order to beat strong players.

Here is a more complex example that features a stunning tactic. It also highlights some of the points I have made over the last few pages. **1 d4 ♘f6 2 c4 c5 3 d5 e5 4 ♘c3 d6.**

This looks like a blocked position where not much is going to happen for a while. But tactics are always lurking just beneath the surface. With **5 ♗g5** White creates a pin. However, after **5...♗e7** White has set himself up for a few headaches. Do you see Black's threat? If not, read on...

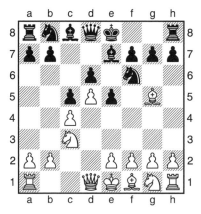

Now the obvious move 6 e4? is bad. Why? First of all, Black has the 'Sicilian Unpin' 6...♘xe4 7 ♗xe7 ♘xc3!, an idea we see in Trap 35. However, it is complicated, and there is something better and clearer. The 'elastic band' move 6...♘xd5! 7 ♗xe7 ♘xe7! cleanly picks off a pawn.

But after **6 ♘f3** does the elastic band still work?

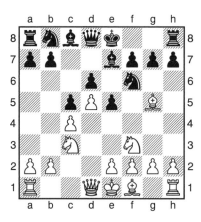

No, because the knight on f3 proves very 'relevant': now 6...♘xd5?? loses to 7 ♘xd5 ♗xg5 8 ♘xg5 ♕xg5 and with the queen dragged away from d8, 9 ♘c7+ is a deadly knight fork.

So after **6...♘a6 7 e4** we have the same question again. Yes, 7...♘xd5 is possible here, but gives Black no advantage because of 8 ♕xd5 ♗xg5 9 ♘xg5 ♕xg5 10 ♕xd6. So Black plays **7...0-0**, when **8 ♗e2??** looks like routine development but is a fatal error. **8...♘xd5!** has an incredible appearance:

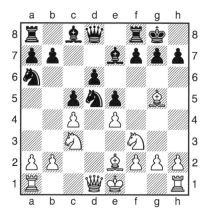

Black boldly takes a pawn that is defended four times! Now **9 ♗xe7 ♘xe7!** is the 'elastic band' move, snapping back to save the knight from capture. After **9 ♕xd5 ♗xg5 10 ♘xg5 ♕xg5 11 ♕xd6 ♖d8** White is lucky not to be losing on the spot. The only way to save the white queen is **12 h4! ♕xh4! 13 ♖xh4 ♖xd6**, but it leaves him a pawn down.

Let's end with a nice piece of opening tactics, which shows the depth and beauty that is possible within the first dozen moves: **1 e4 e5 2 ♘c3 ♘f6 3 ♗c4 ♘c6 4 d3 ♗c5 5 f4 0-0 6 ♘f3 ♘g4** (Black greedily eyes a fork on f2, but this move isn't bad) **7 ♘g5 d5! 8 ♘xd5!**.

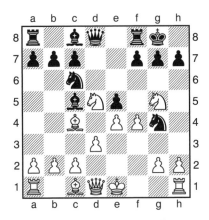

Now 8...exf4 intending ...♘ce5 gives Black fair chances. Instead with **8...h6?** Black goes wrong, but the reason is very hard to see. With **9 f5!** White starts a remarkable sequence. **9...♘f2 10 ♕h5! ♘xh1** (10...hxg5 11 ♗xg5 gives White a winning attack because 11...f6 allows instant mate) **11 f6! ♘d4** (11...hxg5 12 ♕xg5! g6 13 ♕h6 and ♕g7# is a standard mating pattern).

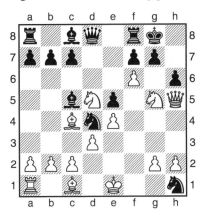

Now comes a theme that you might call 'That *Thing* on g6' since the queen suddenly appears in front of the king as a complete shock: **12 ♕g6!! ♘xc2+ 13 ♔f1**. White threatens ♕xg7# and ♕h7#, while **13...fxg6**

14 ♘e7++ (*double check!*) **14...♔h8 15 ♘xg6#** is a beautiful mate with two knights and a bishop. White is a queen and rook down here but wins – there is much more to chess than counting pieces!

This game is from a team event in England and was won by another player I knew from local chess in the southwest.

The 100 Traps

As you work your way through the book, you will notice that the complexity increases. The later sections have more difficult ideas, more variations and moves that are harder to see. Here's the breakdown:

Section 1 (Traps 1-20): Basic Tactics: Traps based around a single tactic, without much complicated calculation needed. The main themes are mate, double attack, assault on f7, and tricks with pawns.

Section 2 (Traps 21-56): Combining Ideas: Traps with one tactic setting up another or where the defender has more resources of his own. There are longer variations to calculate or harder moves to see. We have similar themes to those in Section 1, but also a lot about trapped pieces (including queens), pins, discoveries, and attacks on kings that have just castled.

Section 3 (Traps 57-100): Advanced Concepts: Several themes at play at once or much more 'fight' in the position. The later sections feature general topics and themes for the defender.

If a section seems too difficult for you, don't panic. Look at the diagrams, play through only the moves given **in bold** and try to understand the main point I am explaining in the text. You can come back to it later and examine the moves in more detail then.

TRAP 1 — Smothered Mate with a Pin

A shocking raid by a knight with air support from a queen

In our earliest chess lessons we learn about the smothered mate, where a knight checkmates a king boxed in by its own pieces. A pure smothered mate is unlikely in the opening, but all it takes is a key pawn to be pinned, and suddenly the bomb can drop.

This simple example has claimed many victims: **1 e4 c6 2 ♘f3 d5 3 ♘c3 dxe4 4 ♘xe4 ♘d7 5 ♕e2**. After this odd-looking move, Black should stop and think what White is up to. If he plays his planned move, he learns too late: **5...♘gf6?? 6 ♘d6#**.

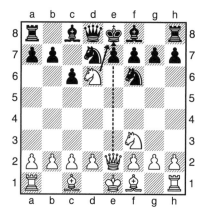

The queen pins Black's e7-pawn, so it's mate and the game is already over! Black could have avoided this disaster by playing 5...♘df6, when his knights look a little odd, but so does the white queen on e2, blocking the development of the bishop on f1.

This trick can also be more deeply hidden: **1 d4 ♘f6 2 c4 e5** (this gambit is called the Budapest Defence) **3 dxe5 ♘g4 4 ♗f4 ♘c6 5 ♘f3 ♗b4+ 6 ♘bd2 ♕e7** (Black is just trying to get his sacrificed pawn back) **7 a3 ♘gxe5**. It seems like Black has forgotten about his attacked bishop, but no: **8 axb4??** is a fatal mistake.

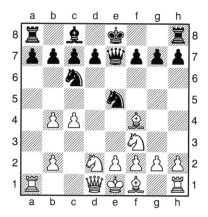

Now **8...♘d3#** is a snap mate!

The opening line **1 c4 e5 2 ♘c3 ♘f6 3 ♘f3 ♘c6 4 g3 ♘d4** has been played at top grandmaster level. The point is seen after **5 ♘xe5?! ♕e7**.

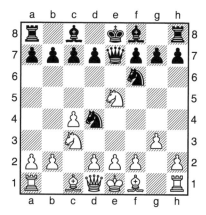

Now the obvious knight retreat **6 ♘d3??** allows mate by **6...♘f3#**!

14

Mate Out of the Blue

Strategy matters, but mate matters more

A sudden checkmate can rip a game away from its apparently logical course. It might seem a random and unfair event, but we must always be on the lookout for danger to both kings. In our two examples here, neither king looked in any trouble until a move or two from the end.

1 e4 ♘c6 2 d4 d5 3 exd5 ♕xd5 4 ♘f3 ♗g4 5 ♘c3 ♗xf3?! 6 ♘xd5 ♗xd1 7 ♘xc7+ ♔d8 8 ♘xa8 ♗xc2 is a very risky opening line for Black. He has started a fierce tactical battle, which is generally unwise for the player who is starting out a step behind. Now 9 d5! is the best way to give Black problems. But a game from 1927, between Bildhauer and Janny, shows that there are dangers for White too. After **9 ♗f4 ♘xd4 10 ♘c7??**, Black won with the surprising **10...e5!**.

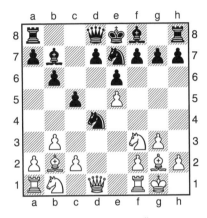

After **10 ♘xd4 ♗xg2 11 ♘b5!** Black resigned in a high-level game.

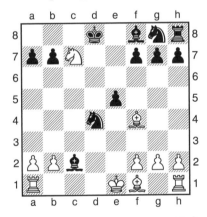

Why is this so strong? Because **11 ♗xe5? ♗b4#** is a sudden mate!

Here is another game where mate appears out of nowhere: **1 e4 c5 2 ♘f3 e6 3 b3 ♘f6 4 e5 ♘d5 5 ♗b2 b6 6 g3 ♗b7 7 ♗g2 ♘c6 8 0-0 ♘de7 9 d4 ♘xd4??**. Black avoids his knight being pinned on the long h1-a8 diagonal after 9...cxd4 10 ♘xd4, but this is a minor problem compared to what happened next.

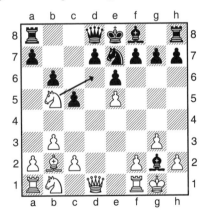

If Black rescues his bishop or plays **11...♗xf1**, White will mate with **12 ♘d6#**. If he defends against the mate with a move such as **11...♘g6**, White answers **12 ♔xg2**, keeping an extra piece.

TRAP 3 Mating-Net with Bishop and Knight

Catch the king napping with this great set-play

This checkmate can arise early in the opening if a player has fianchettoed his king's bishop but not protected a few key squares carefully enough. The crowning blow is a queen sacrifice.

1 e4 ♘f6 2 ♘c3 d5 3 exd5 ♘xd5 and now **4 ♘ge2?!** seems a logical way to prepare to fianchetto the king's bishop, but Black has a good reply based on a clever tactic: **4...♘c6!**. Very alert. We see why next move. **5 g3?** (5 ♘xd5 ♕xd5 leaves Black with a grip on the centre, while after 5 d4 ♘xc3 6 bxc3 e5 the white pawns are feeble) **5...♗g4! 6 ♗g2 ♘d4!**. Eyeing the weak light squares around White's king. But what if White takes the piece? **7 ♗xd5?** (7 h3 ♘xc3 8 dxc3 ♘f3+ 9 ♗xf3 ♕xd1+ 10 ♔xd1 ♗xf3 is horrible for White, but he can try to defend).

trappy move; 5 ♘xd4 is simpler, and gives White a good game) **5...♗g7 6 ♗g5**.

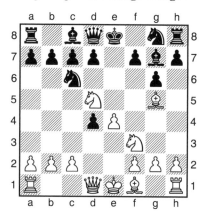

Now 6...♘ce7 is best. Black keeps control of f6 and can play ...c6 to force the knight back from d5. If Black doesn't know the mating-net, he might play **6...♘ge7??**, losing to **7 ♘xd4**, when **7...♗xd4 8 ♕xd4! ♘xd4 9 ♘f6+ ♔f8 10 ♗h6#** is the familiar mate.

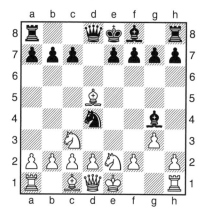

7...♕xd5! 8 ♘xd5 (allowing mate, but White is lost anyway) **8...♘f3+ 9 ♔f1 ♗h3#**.

There are various other openings where this idea comes into play. **1 e4 e5 2 ♘f3 ♘c6 3 ♘c3 g6** (this is one form of the Three Knights Game; 3...♘f6 is considered safer for Black, and is called, you guessed it, the Four Knights Game) **4 d4 exd4 5 ♘d5** (a

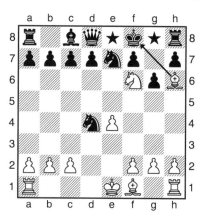

TRAP 4 — Snap Mate with Two Bishops

The bishops can strike from near or far

Two bishops control a lot of squares between them – enough to mate a king on their own as long as a few extra squares are blocked.

1 e4 c6 2 ♘f3 d5 3 ♘c3 ♗g4 4 h3 ♗xf3 5 ♕xf3 ♘f6 6 d4 dxe4 7 ♕e3 ♘d5 8 ♕xe4 ♘xc3 9 bxc3 e6 10 ♖b1 ♕c8 11 ♗d3 ♘d7 12 ♗g5 h6??. Black wants to force the bishop to retreat and then develop his kingside, but misses a snap mate.

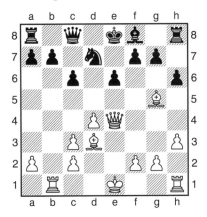

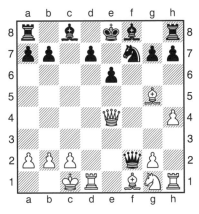

13 ♕xe6+! fxe6 14 ♗g6#. This mating pattern can occur in many forms.

Here's another example, with a different structure and an open centre: **1 d4 f5 2 e4 fxe4 3 ♘c3 ♘f6 4 ♗g5 ♘c6 5 d5 ♘e5 6 ♕e2!? ♘f7 7 h4 c6 8 0-0-0 ♘xd5** (8...cxd5 9 ♘xd5 e6 is safer) **9 ♘xd5 cxd5 10 ♖xd5 ♕b6?! 11 ♕xe4 e6 12 ♖d1**. Daring play by both sides has led to a wild position. Black must be careful. 12...♕c6 seeks a queen exchange and to develop with ...b6 and ...♗b7. But **12...♕xf2??** (played in a game in Spain) gives up control of some key squares. The queen was guarding e6 and b5, and White shows in brilliant fashion why they matter:

13 ♕xe6+! forces mate in two more moves: **13...dxe6 14 ♗b5+ ♗d7 15 ♗xd7#**.

A version of the mate against a king that has castled queenside is called Boden's Mate: **1 e4 d5 2 exd5 ♕xd5 3 ♘c3 ♕a5 4 d4 ♘f6 5 ♗c4 ♗f5 6 ♘f3 c6 7 0-0 e6 8 ♗f4 ♘bd7 9 ♖e1 0-0-0 10 a3 ♗g4 11 h3 ♗xf3? 12 ♕xf3 ♕h5?** (fatally abandoning the queenside) **13 ♕xc6+! bxc6 14 ♗a6#**.

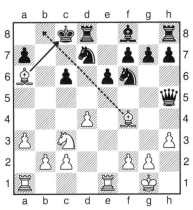

TRAP 5 — Bungled Philidor's Legacy

Yes, I'm going to mate! Oh no...

'Philidor's Legacy' is an amazing mating idea that is taught to almost every beginner. It features a double check and a queen sacrifice to force a smothered mate.

When this mating idea appears early in the game, it is usually when a king has just castled but is very poorly guarded by its own pieces. Let's look at an example from a game played in Russia. **1 e4 e5 2 ♘f3 ♘c6 3 d4 exd4 4 ♘xd4 ♘f6 5 ♘c3 ♗b4 6 ♘xc6 bxc6 7 ♕f3 h6 8 a3 ♗xc3+ 9 ♕xc3 0-0 10 ♗d3 ♖e8 11 f3 d5 12 ♕xc6?**. White grabs a pawn but leaves his king unprotected. **12...dxe4! 13 fxe4 ♘xe4! 14 0-0 ♕d4+ 15 ♔h1 ♗d7!** (15...♘f2+ 16 ♖xf2 ♕xf2?? allows 17 ♕xe8#) **16 ♕c4**.

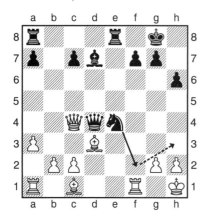

16...♘f2+ 17 ♔g1 ♘h3++ 18 ♔h1 ♕g1+! 19 ♖xg1 ♘f2#.

However, I was shocked to find so many instances of a bungled Philidor's Legacy. In well over a dozen games, players – including some masters – got as far as making the queen sacrifice only to find that there was no mate! How embarrassing! I must confess that

I also did this once – I was about ten years old and it was in a lightning tournament, but still felt pretty silly. Imagine what it must have felt like for the master who made this blunder in a European junior championship game: **1 c4 g6 2 g3 ♗g7 3 ♗g2 ♘f6 4 ♘c3 0-0 5 e4 e5 6 ♘ge2 d6 7 0-0 c6 8 d3 ♘a6 9 f4?! ♕b6+ 10 ♔h1 ♘g4 11 ♘a4? ♘f2+ 12 ♔g1**.

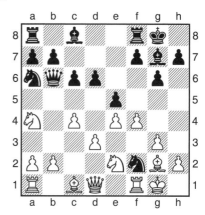

12...♘h3++ (12...♘xd1+ 13 ♘xb6 axb6 14 ♖xd1 ♘c5 is excellent for Black, but why play this when you think you have a forced mate in three moves?) **13 ♔h1 ♕g1+??**. Black resigned here before White could play **14 ♘xg1**. So remember that Philidor's Legacy may not work when there is an additional piece covering the g1-square! And always check 'simple obvious winning moves'. 14 ♖xg1?? ♘f2# was of course Black's intended point.

A Junior Chess Special

One weakness, one sacrifice, one point

This isn't an idea you'll see much in master and grandmaster games, but it crops up all the time in junior chess. It happens when Black has castled and played ...h6, White sacrifices a bishop or knight on h6 and picks off a loose knight on f6. This tactic gains at least a pawn, and shatters the kingside defences too. Strong players tend not to fall for such simple tactics. They also are very wary of making weakening pawn moves in front of their king.

1 e4 e5 2 ♘c3 ♘f6 3 ♗c4 ♘c6 4 d3 ♗c5 5 ♘ge2? h6? (both players miss 5...♘g4!, when 6 0-0? ♕h4! is winning for Black) **6 h3 0-0 7 ♘g3 ♘e7 8 ♕f3**. Neither side has played the opening well. The moves by the h-pawns were unnecessary and weakening. Both players have spent time on knight manoeuvres when they still had other pieces to develop. Anyway, White's last move created a threat... **8...d6??** ...which Black misses. 8...♘g6 is correct, when Black is safe.

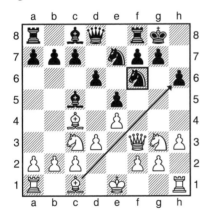

With **9 ♗xh6!** White *overloads* Black's g-pawn: if it takes the bishop, it no longer defends the knight on f6. After **9...gxh6?** Black loses more than just one pawn, but there was no good answer. **10 ♕xf6** threatens ♘h5 and ♕g7#, so Black resigned in a junior game played in the Faeroe Islands. While this exact position may be unique to

that game, similar sequences have decided junior games the world over.

In the next example, it is the knight that is sacrificed on h6. **1 e4 e5 2 ♘f3 ♘c6 3 ♗c4 ♘f6 4 d3 h6**. This move has been played by some extremely strong players, but it weakens the kingside, and care is needed to avoid this becoming a real problem. **5 ♗b3 ♗c5 6 c3 ♗b6 7 ♘bd2 d6 8 ♘f1 ♗g4 9 h3 ♗h5**. Misplacing the bishop. Black really doesn't want to exchange it for a knight. **10 ♘g3 ♗xf3?! 11 ♕xf3 0-0 12 ♘f5 ♘e7?**. White already has a strong attack, but this allows an immediate breakthrough.

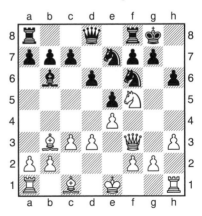

13 ♘xh6+! gxh6 14 ♕xf6. Once again, White is winning much more than a pawn, with ♗xh6 a threat. **14...♘g6?** allows simply **15 ♕xg6+** due to the pin, but that didn't stop it being played in a game in France.

TRAP 7   Double Attacks with the Queen

Got weaknesses? The queen will find them

Like no other piece, the queen radiates power in all directions. So it is no surprise that it can produce all manner of double attacks, both on its own against loose pieces, and especially with a helping hand from other pieces. Here are a couple of striking yet typical examples.

We start with a common idea in the French Defence. **1 e4 e6 2 d4 d5 3 ♘c3 dxe4 4 ♘xe4 ♘d7 5 ♘f3 ♘gf6 6 ♗g5 ♗e7 7 ♗xf6 ♘xf6 8 ♗d3 0-0 9 ♕e2**. White has no particular threat here. But that doesn't mean Black can be careless! **9...b6??** gives White an extra target.

have much real purpose. This should make Black wonder what the idea might be. **8...0-0 9 ♘e5 ♘xe5?? 10 dxe5 ♘d7?** (10...♘e4 is relatively best, even though it loses a pawn for nothing; 10...♘h5 11 ♗xe7 ♕xe7 12 g4 leaves the knight trapped) **11 ♕h4.**

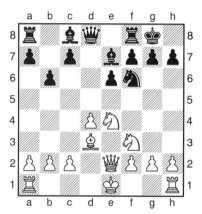

After **10 ♘xf6+ ♗xf6 11 ♕e4** we have a decisive double attack. Black is either mated by ♕xh7# or loses the rook on a8. This has occurred in dozens of games, and is also an example of the *Uncompleted Fianchetto*, a theme we discuss in Trap 72.

Our second example is from a queen's pawn opening, the Torre Attack. **1 d4 ♘f6 2 ♗g5 e6 3 ♘f3 ♗e7 4 ♘bd2 d5 5 e3 c5 6 c3 ♘bd7 7 ♗d3 b6 8 ♕a4**. Apart from the trap we are about to see, this queen move doesn't

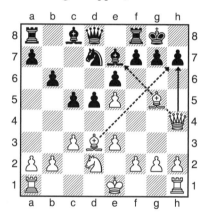

White has a deadly double threat: mate on h7 or taking the bishop on e7.

Somehow this idea must be hard to see. It has claimed more and much stronger victims than you would expect for a fairly simple tactic kicked off by a suspicious-looking queen move. Perhaps players assume that White's plan is to probe the queenside and forget about the 'long' move of the queen from a4 to h4. At the point when they need to picture that key queen move, the fourth rank is closed off by the white pawn on d4.

TRAP 8   Simple Queen Win with ♗xh7+

This one has been breaking players' hearts for decades

This theme generally occurs at the end of the opening or in the early middlegame as pawn exchanges open the centre. Many players have lost queens to this idea, so please note it well!

Our first example comes from a high-level grandmaster game: **1 d4 ♘f6 2 c4 e6 3 ♘c3 ♗b4 4 e3 0-0 5 ♗d3 d5 6 ♘f3 ♘c6 7 0-0 dxc4 8 ♗xc4 ♗d6 9 ♗b5 e5 10 ♗xc6 exd4 11 exd4 bxc6 12 ♗g5 ♖e8 13 ♕d3 c5**. The play has been fairly normal so far, but with his next move, a Romanian grandmaster made a terrible mistake: **14 dxc5??**.

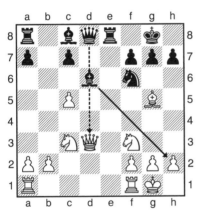

He must have expected Black to recapture with 14...♗xc5??, but his opponent, Bobby Fischer, was not one to miss **14...♗xh2+!**. The discovered attack wins the white queen. This was an unusual case, as even at amateur level, players don't normally miss such simple tactics. This theme generally occurs after a sequence of exchanges ends with an undefended queen in the middle of the board.

Here is a more typical example: **1 e4 c5** (this is the Sicilian Defence) **2 ♘f3 a6 3 d4 cxd4 4 ♘xd4 ♘f6 5 ♗d3 e5 6 ♘f3 ♘c6 7 0-0 ♗c5 8 h3 0-0 9 ♘c3**. White has played

very cautiously, and Black should have no problems. One of the first strategic ideas players learn in the Sicilian is that Black's ...d5 pawn-break is often strong. However, the tactics have to work, and here they don't: **9...d5??** is a terrible mistake.

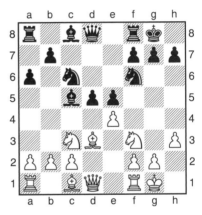

10 exd5 ♘xd5? (now Black loses a piece, but by this point he had no good options) **11 ♘xd5 ♕xd5 12 ♗xh7+ ♔xh7 13 ♕xd5** and White has an extra queen. The general idea has occurred in many games: exchanges on d5 leave a queen on that square which is picked off thanks to a ♗xh7+ tactic. Many years ago, I myself nearly threw away a junior championship in this way, but fortunately my opponent missed the win.

How do you avoid becoming the next victim? You need to be well aware of the idea so that you see it far in advance. Then you won't start the disastrous series of exchanges in the first place.

TRAP 9 — Attack on f7: No Way to Defend

Why complicate? Just stroll in and take the thing!

Some tactics are too simple to be considered tactics by most books! What if we just attack a key pawn, and there is no way to defend it? This can and does happen, and it decides many games.

1 e4 d5 2 ♘c3 dxe4 3 ♘xe4 and with **3...e5** Black grabs central space but is inviting hand-to-hand combat. After **4 ♗c4** White has rapid development and is eyeing f7. That's two red flags, so Black must be alert and check everything carefully before choosing his move. **4...♗e7??** Or not! Players learn not to fear cheap threats of mate on f7 in the opening, but that's only because there is normally a good defence to them. Here there isn't! 4...♘f6? is also bad, because of the simple 5 ♘g5. 4...♘c6 is a good way to prepare ...♗e7.

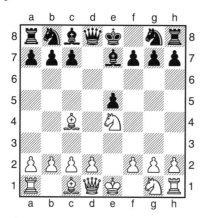

5 ♕h5! ♘h6 6 d3!. The threat of ♗xh6 is the finishing touch. Black will lose material and have a broken position. Instead 6 ♕xe5? lets Black off the hook, since after 6...0-0 he can expect some compensation for the pawn due to White's now disorganized pieces.

In our second example, the threat is just as simple, but better hidden. **1 e4 e5 2 ♘f3 d6** (this opening is called Philidor's Defence) **3 ♗c4** (3 d4 ♘d7 4 ♗c4 c6 is the same) **3...c6 4 d4 ♘d7** and now **5 c3** is a sly move. It looks like White is just supporting his d4-pawn, but there is a far nastier idea. **5...♗e7??** (5...♘gf6 is a better defence, when Black can avoid any immediate disaster: 6 ♘g5 d5!, 6 ♕b3 ♕e7 or 6 dxe5 ♘xe4) **6 ♕b3!**.

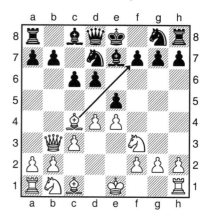

It's that simple. There is no good way to prevent ♗xf7+. 6...♘h6? 7 ♗xh6 obviously doesn't help Black at all, while 6...♘gf6? is simple surrender – some games had a nice finish after 7 ♗xf7+ ♔f8 8 ♘g5 ♕b6 9 ♘e6+! ♔xf7 10 ♘g5++, a double check that forces mate. After **6...d5 7 exd5** Black has tried various moves, but the basic truth is that he is a pawn down and desperately trying to avoid losing even more. One game went **7...b5 8 ♗d3 exd4 9 cxd4 c5 10 ♗xb5 ♘f6 11 ♗c6** and Black could only hope for a miracle.

TRAP 10   f7: Sacrifice or Simply Attack

Violence is the last refuge of... those who want to win chess games!

In some positions, all we need to do is attack f7 (or f2), but in other cases – even with just a slight change in the position – we might need to sacrifice.

Take a look at **1 ♘f3 ♘f6 2 c4 e6 3 g3 d5 4 ♗g2 dxc4**. After **5 ♘a3 c6?! 6 ♘xc4 b5 7 ♘ce5**, the careless move **7...♗b7??** allows the simple **8 ♘g5**.

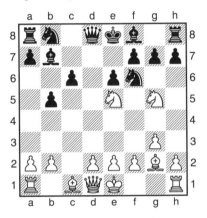

There is no way to defend f7 – no sacrifice is needed to win here! But think about the position after **5 0-0 a6 6 ♘a3 c5?! 7 ♘xc4 b5 8 ♘ce5 ♗b7??**.

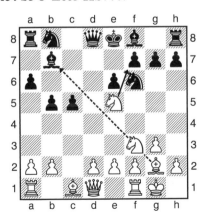

Then 9 ♘g5? is no good due to 9...♗xg2 10 ♔xg2 ♕d5+. But there is another way: **9 ♘xf7! ♔xf7 10 ♘g5+**. The knight check discovers an attack on the b7-bishop. After **10...♔e7 11 ♗xb7** White is a pawn up and Black's position is in ruins.

An attack on f2 can suddenly appear when it looks like both sides are quietly developing: **1 e4 e6 2 d3 d5 3 ♘d2 ♘f6 4 ♘gf3** (4 g3 dxe4 5 dxe4 ♗c5 6 ♘gf3?? ♘g4 is another way for White to fall victim to the same idea) **4...♗c5** and now **5 g3??** has been played more than 50 times. Perhaps it seems not much is going on in the position, so White just continues with his planned development. But then comes **5...dxe4!** (not 5...♘g4? 6 d4).

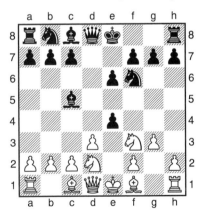

After **6 dxe4?! ♘g4** the crude attack on f2 not only wins a pawn but shatters White's position. White can limit the damage to a pawn with 6 ♘g5 or 6 ♘xe4 ♘xe4 7 dxe4 ♗xf2+!, but it's a horrible way to start a game.

A Violent Unpin

Discovering how to turn a pin on its head

Pinning a piece against a queen can be double-edged. Suppose a knight is pinned by a bishop. If the knight can suddenly give check, then the queen can take the bishop. This is a very common theme that has helped win thousands of games. In this section we look at a couple of common set-ups, but remember this is a general idea rather than a specific trap. We shall see more examples of it later in the book.

We shall look at the tricky opening line **1 e4 c6 2 d4 d5 3 f3 dxe4 4 fxe4 e5 5 ♘f3** in more depth in Trap 75. Here we shall just see what happens if Black carelessly plays his two most active-looking developing moves: **5...♗g4 6 ♗c4 ♘f6??**. Black has pinned the white knight and attacked the central e4-pawn. But there is a problem. Instead both 6...♘d7 and 6...♗h5 defend against White's threat. **7 ♗xf7+! ♔xf7 8 ♘xe5+.**

This tactical idea can work in many different structures. As long as White can follow up the sacrifice on f7 with a knight check that wins a bishop on g4, it can be devastating, even if the rest of the pieces are on other squares. Here is one from the Sicilian Defence: **1 e4 c5 2 ♘c3 d6 3 f4 g6 4 ♘f3 ♗g7 5 ♗c4 ♘c6 6 0-0 ♗g4??** (if Black wants to put the bishop here, he should play 6...♘f6 first).

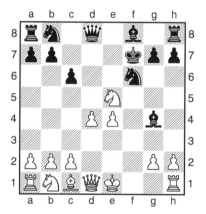

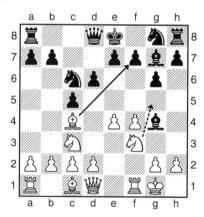

The g4-bishop is defended once but attacked twice. After **8...♔e8 9 ♘xg4 ♘xg4 10 ♕xg4 ♕xd4 11 ♘c3** White is a pawn up. He can also expect to launch an overwhelming attack on the black king, which – let's not forget – cannot castle any more.

7 ♗xf7+! wins a pawn and forces the black king to wander. After **7...♔xf7** the knight cannot fork on e5, but **8 ♘g5+** is good enough since the bishop is undefended on g4. **8...♔e8 9 ♕xg4** is a position White should win with good play.

More Disasters on f2/f7

A club-player version and a master version!

The sacrifice on f7 to unleash a discovered attack is so important and so often missed that we should look at some more examples. First of all, let's not forget that Black can also use this idea – that is, against White's f2-square.

1 d4 ♘f6 2 c4 e5 3 d5?!. Hoping to play it safe, White declines Black's gambit. But some gambits really have to be taken. This move wastes time and lets Black develop his pieces to ideal squares. **3...♗c5 4 ♗g5??**. White pins the knight, again hoping to limit Black's tactical options. This move has been played hundreds of times, but is a catastrophic blunder. 4 ♘f3 d6 5 ♗g5?? ♗xf2+! 6 ♔xf2 ♘e4+ is another version of the idea.

mission since 6...♕xg5 defends the knight) **6...♕xg5** and Black is a pawn up with a great position.

That trap has claimed vast numbers of victims at club level, but not at master level. Surely that's because masters would never miss such a simple idea? However... **1 d4 ♘f6 2 c4 e6 3 ♘c3 ♗b4 4 ♕c2 c5 5 dxc5 0-0 6 a3 ♗xc5** is a quiet-looking position in an opening called the Nimzo-Indian.

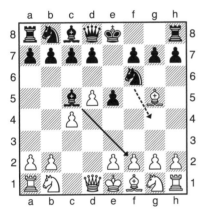

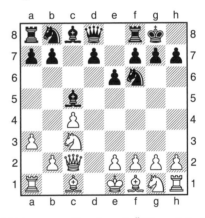

4...♗xf2+!. Black seizes his opportunity. 4...♘e4! is also strong: if White grabs the queen with 5 ♗xd8?, he is mated on the spot by 5...♗xf2#. After 5 ♗e3 ♗xe3 6 fxe3, White hasn't lost material yet, but his position is a wreck. **5 ♔xf2 ♘g4+!**. Only this knight check is good! 5...♘e4+? 6 ♔e3 isn't clear, since 6...♘xg5? 7 h4 traps the knight and after 6...♕xg5+ 7 ♔xe4 the king survives his trip to the centre of the board – this time! **6 ♔e1** (6 ♔g3? is now a suicide

White normally plays 7 ♘f3 and decides on his next move whether to play ♗f4 or ♗g5. But the immediate **7 ♗g5??** is a terrible mistake because of **7...♗xf2+! 8 ♔xf2 ♘g4+**, winning a pawn and leaving White's position a broken mess. Oddly, this version of the idea *has* claimed some very strong victims, including masters. That's true in both this exact position and in very similar ones. If you think there aren't tactics, you are far more likely to miss them!

TRAP 13   Failed ♗xf7+ Discovery Trick

Yes, it is legal for a queen to take a defended knight

Hold your horses! (And your bishops!) Before you start smacking that bishop down on f7, check it actually works.

1 e4 d5 2 exd5 ♕xd5 3 ♘c3 ♕a5 4 ♗c4 ♘f6 5 d4 c6 6 ♘f3 and now **6...♗g4** is a normal developing move, but it invites a blunder that has claimed more victims than most 'real' traps have. With **7 ♗xf7+??** White thinks he has caught his opponent with a knight-fork trick. If he's right, he will be winning. In moments like this, pause to make sure it isn't you who has missed something important. Here he has. **7...♔xf7 8 ♘e5+.**

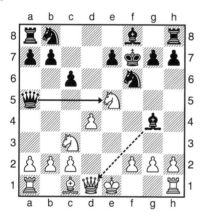

If the black king retreats, White takes on g4 with a huge advantage. But **8...♕xe5+! 9 dxe5 ♗xd1** leaves Black a piece up. There is nothing complicated about this sequence, yet it has occurred in more than 30 games, including ones between high-rated players. Similar ideas in other openings have claimed many victims too. We are so used to ignoring moves that leave the queen *en prise* ('in a position to be taken') that we mentally filter them out, even when they win on the spot.

In one of my first club matches I made a similar mistake: **1 d4 d5 2 c4 dxc4 3 e4 e5 4 ♘f3 exd4 5 ♗xc4 ♘c6 6 0-0** is a well-known opening line where White is a pawn down but has very active pieces. **6...♗g4?** is not a good reply.

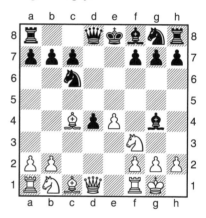

Black's careless bishop move can be punished by 7 ♕b3!, attacking both f7 and b7. However, I played instead **7 ♗xf7+?? ♔xf7 8 ♘g5+**, when Black could have replied **8...♕xg5!**. Again, the queen captures an apparently well-defended knight, but it wins because White's queen is under attack too. 9 ♗xg5 ♗xd1 10 ♖xd1 leaves Black a piece up, 9 f3 ♕g6 10 fxg4+ ♔e8 gives White nothing like enough for the piece, and 9 ♕b3+ ♗e6 10 ♕xb7 doesn't help because White is two pieces down. Fortunately my opponent missed his chance and after 8...♔e8?? 9 ♕xg4 I won the game quickly. But I had learnt a valuable lesson!

The *Other* Weakest Square

The c7-square can collapse just as dramatically as f7

We have already seen f7 – defended only by the king – coming under fire. But if c7 can be attacked by two pieces, the outcome can be just as devastating.

In this short game, Black didn't see any danger until it was too late: **1 e4 e5 2 ♘f3 ♘c6 3 d4 exd4 4 ♘xd4 d6**. Black does better to play 4...♘f6 and develop his kingside. **5 ♘c3 g6 6 ♘d5**. Already the position is tricky for Black, as 6...♘f6 7 ♗g5 leaves him pinned and under pressure. But that is still better than what happened: **6...♗g7?? 7 ♘b5**.

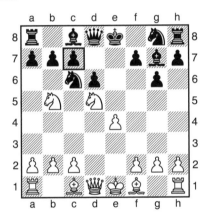

Black can't defend the c7-pawn a second time. As a knight landing there would win a rook, Black can only limit the damage to two pawns and a wrecked position.

Your author managed a similar quick victory at a tournament in Wales: **1 d4 g6 2 e4 ♗g7 3 c4 d6 4 ♘c3 ♘c6 5 ♗e3 e5 6 ♘ge2 f5 7 exf5 gxf5 8 f4 exd4 9 ♘xd4**. White isn't threatening much here, so Black decided to play an active move: **9...♕e7??**. But White now gets a free move by attacking the queen: **10 ♘d5 ♕f7 11 ♘b5**.

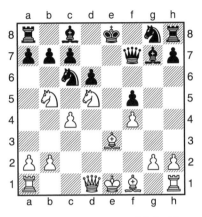

The c7-pawn falls, and with it d6 too.

In our final example, the queen supports a knight: **1 e4 e5 2 ♘f3 ♘c6 3 ♘c3 ♗c5 4 ♘xe5 ♘xe5 5 d4 ♗xd4?! 6 ♕xd4 ♕f6??**. Black threatens 7...♘f3+, but there is a problem: **7 ♘b5! ♔d8 8 ♕c5!**.

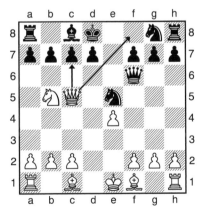

Threatening not just 9 ♕xc7+ but also 9 ♕f8#. There's no good defence.

TRAP 15   OMG Trap in Practice

Every dog has its day

As mentioned in the Introduction, after **1 e4 e5 2 ♘f3 ♘c6 3 ♗c4, 3...♘d4?** is an example of a bad move that sets a trap. But we can still learn from it.

The point is **4 ♘xe5?? ♛g5 5 ♘xf7? ♛xg2 6 ♖f1 ♛xe4+ 7 ♗e2 ♘f3#**. But 4 ♘xd4 and 4 0-0 are very good for White. You shouldn't be tempted to play moves like 3...♘d4? – you should always assume the opponent is going to play the best move, rather than hoping he will fall into a trap. However, there are some opening lines where this idea can occur without it being a crude trap. For instance, in the Two Knights Defence, after **1 e4 e5 2 ♘f3 ♘c6 3 ♗c4 ♘f6 4 ♘g5 d5 5 exd5**, 5...♘d4 is an interesting alternative to the main line, 5...♘a5. One point is shown by **6 d6 ♛xd6 7 ♘xf7??** (instead of this greedy move, the sensible 7 d3 gives White a decent position).

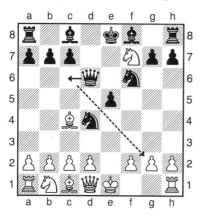

After **7...♛c6 8 ♘xh8 ♛xg2** White realizes to his horror that he has fallen into the same idea as the OMG Trap, and is hopelessly lost; e.g., **9 ♖f1 ♛e4+ 10 ♗e2 ♘f3#**.

Another way for the OMG theme to arise in 'real' games is **1 e4 e5 2 ♘f3 ♘c6 3 ♗b5 ♘d4 4 ♗c4 ♗c5 5 ♘xe5?**. Black even has a useful extra move here, but White's sense of danger might be reduced since Black hasn't played an obviously suspicious-looking move. **5...♛g5** gives White real problems, but oddly the bishop being on c5 actually offers White more chances here.

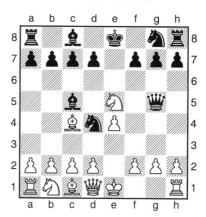

We already know **6 ♘xf7?? ♛xg2 7 ♖f1 ♛xe4+ 8 ♗e2 ♘f3#**. Instead 6 ♘g4? loses to 6...d5!, attacking two pieces (on c4 and g4). 6 ♗xf7+ ♚d8 7 0-0 ♛xe5 8 c3 ♘f6 9 cxd4 ♗xd4 10 d3 ♖f8 gives Black a strong attack. White's best option is **6 0-0 ♛xe5 7 c3** because if the knight retreats, White will make a *pawn fork* by playing d4. **7...♘f6! 8 cxd4 ♗xd4** gives Black an excellent game, though he is far from winning.

TRAP 16   Trapping the Queen with ♗xf7+

Neglect e6 at your queen's peril

A devastating raid by bishop and knight can crop up after just four moves. All it takes is for the black queen to be short of squares and the white pieces to be in position.

After **1 e4 g6 2 d4 ♗g7 3 ♘f3 d6 4 ♗c4** the blunder **4...♘d7??** has been played in a remarkable number of games, and by some strong players (1 d4 d6 2 ♘f3 ♘d7 3 e4 g6 4 ♗c4 ♗g7?? is another move-order). Why? Black's moves all look logical in themselves; the problem is purely tactical. White's 4th move didn't actually threaten anything, so Black perhaps felt he had a free choice of developing moves.

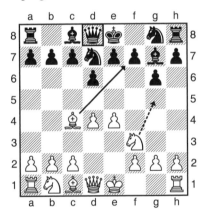

5 ♗xf7+!. After just five moves, and without playing anything obviously absurd, Black is completely lost. **5...♔xf7** (5...♔f8 avoids losing the queen, but Black has lost a vital pawn and his king is hopelessly exposed) **6 ♘g5+ ♔e8** (6...♔f6 allows instant mate by 7 ♕f3#, while 6...♔f8 7 ♘e6+ picks off the queen with a knight fork) **7 ♘e6**. This isn't

check, but White wins the queen anyway because it has nowhere to go.

Here is a related example: **1 e4 c5 2 d4 cxd4 3 c3** (this is the Morra Gambit, a trappy opening!) **3...dxc3 4 ♘xc3 ♘c6 5 ♘f3 d6 6 ♗c4 a6 7 0-0 ♘f6 8 h3** (instead of this slow move, Morra experts tell us that 8 ♗f4 is best) **8...g6 9 ♕e2 ♗g7 10 ♖d1**.

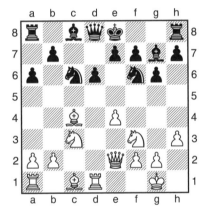

With the d6-pawn pinned, White is now threatening to play e5. **10...♘d7??** is not the way to defend, since it allows the familiar idea: **11 ♗xf7+ ♔xf7 12 ♘g5+ ♔e8** (12...♔g8 is mated by 13 ♕c4+) **13 ♘e6 ♕a5** (13...♕b6 walks into 14 ♘d5) **14 ♘xg7+ ♔f7 15 ♗h6**. Far from being trapped on g7, the white knight will take part in a decisive attack on the black king. 16 ♕c4+ is a huge threat.

TRAP 17   Pin-Based ♘e6

A mid-air bishop drops a bomb on a queen at home

We have already seen some knight invasions on e6 based on a variety of tactical ideas. Next up is a pin on the d7-pawn against the black king. This theme can appear in the Ruy Lopez when there is no pawn on f7.

1 e4 e5 2 ♘f3 ♘c6 3 ♗b5 ♗c5 4 0-0 ♘ge7 5 c3!. Preparing to play d4. **5...f5?!** (5...♗b6 6 d4 exd4 7 cxd4 d5 is better) **6 d4 ♗b6?**.

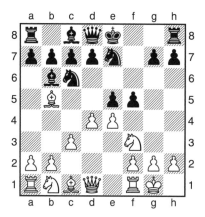

7 d5 fxe4 8 ♘g5 wins a piece, as Black dare not save his knight: **8...♘b8 9 ♘e6**.

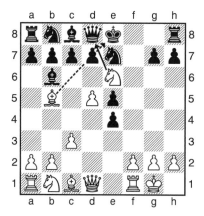

The black queen has no escape and will be captured next move. The e6-knight is invulnerable thanks to the b5-bishop's pin on the d7-pawn.

In our next example, White gives up a bishop in order to land his knight on e6 with devastating effect. **1 e4 e5 2 ♘f3 ♘c6 3 ♗b5 g6 4 d4 exd4 5 c3**. An aggressive gambit: White wants to develop quickly and take advantage of Black's slow play. **5...dxc3 6 ♘xc3 ♗g7 7 ♗g5 ♘ce7?!** (7...♘ge7 8 ♘d5 h6 9 ♗f6 is no fun for Black either) **8 ♕b3 f6?**. Weakening e6, but why should that matter? 8...h6 9 ♗h4 g5 gives Black more hope of getting out of the opening alive.

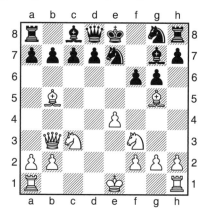

9 e5!? fxg5 10 ♘xg5 ♘h6. White has sacrificed a piece and Black has parried his threat of mate on f7. But now the target is the black queen: **11 ♘e6** and Black's queen is lost. In the last diagram position it looked like the bishop was doing nothing on b5 but it turned out to be perfectly placed.

TRAP 18

A Piece Trapped in Noah's Ark

A bishop drowned under a sturdy wall of pawns

This idea is known as the 'Noah's Ark Trap' due to its old age. But it keeps claiming victims!

1 e4 e5 2 ♘f3 ♘c6 3 ♗b5 a6 4 ♗a4 d6 5 d4 b5 6 ♗b3 ♘xd4 7 ♘xd4 exd4 8 ♕xd4??. With White apparently so active, it's easy to miss that Black can trap the bishop on b3. Instead, both 8 c3 and 8 a4 give White an acceptable game.

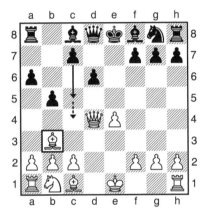

8...c5 9 ♕d5. Threatening mate on f7 and to take the rook on a8. But Black has a good answer: **9...♗e6 10 ♕c6+ ♗d7 11 ♕d5**.

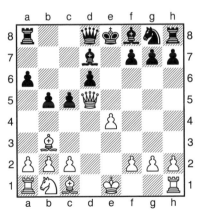

Some games have been agreed drawn here, with Black thinking he has nothing better than repeating with 11...♗e6 12 ♕c6+ ♗d7, etc. However, with the a8-rook defended, he has something far stronger: after **11...c4!** White loses his bishop. This has occurred in about 100 games – and this is just one version of the trap; there are others.

Having seen the basic idea, let's look at a similar position where the theme is more deeply hidden: **1 e4 e5 2 ♘f3 ♘c6 3 ♗b5 a6 4 ♗a4 ♘f6 5 d4 exd4 6 0-0 ♗e7 7 ♖e1** is not a very effective sequence for White, because Black can make use of the Noah's Ark idea to get a good game: **7...b5! 8 ♗b3 d6**.

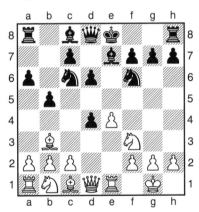

The point is that if White recaptures the pawn with the obvious **9 ♘xd4??**, he loses a piece: **9...♘xd4 10 ♕xd4 c5** and ...c4. Instead of taking on d4, 9 ♗d5 ♘xd5 10 exd5 ♘e5 and 9 c3 dxc3 10 ♘xc3 both leave Black with a good game, but White has fighting chances.

TRAP 19 — Pawns Can Win Pieces!

The humble footsoldier: stabbing, slicing and forking

Even though a pawn is the least powerful piece, it can be very effective at winning enemy pieces. The simplest way is for one pawn to attack two of the opponent's pieces – that is, to *fork* them.

After **1 ♘f3 d5 2 b3 ♗f5 3 ♗b2 e6 4 g3 ♘f6 5 ♗g2 ♘bd7 6 0-0 ♗d6 7 d3 0-0 8 ♘bd2 h6**, the simple-looking move **9 ♖e1**, sliding a rook one square along the back rank, creates a major threat. **9...c6??** (Black fails to spot the danger; 9...♗h7 is the easiest way to avoid losing a piece) **10 e4!**.

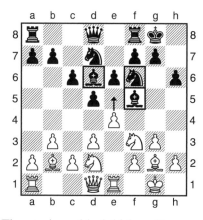

Threatening a black bishop. It can easily step aside, but there is more to come. After **10...♗g4 11 e5!** the pawn forks a black bishop and knight, and Black can't save them both. By putting his rook on e1, White made sure that the pawn would be well-defended. This pawn-fork trick works in many similar positions with the pieces on slightly different squares. We shall see one in the exercises at the end of the book, so remember it well!

But pawns can also help win pieces in other ways too. For instance, they might drive away an important defender, leaving another enemy piece helpless. In the following example, pins also play a major role. **1 c4 c6 2 ♘f3 d5 3 e3 ♘f6 4 ♘c3 ♗g4 5 h3 ♗h5 6 cxd5**. White's play looks harmless... **6...cxd5?**. Falling into a subtle trap. **7 ♕a4+!? ♘bd7 8 ♘e5**.

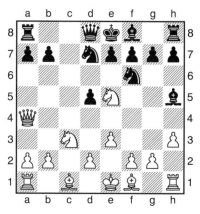

Now 8...a6 attempts to cover b5, but this proves irrelevant after 9 ♘xd7 ♕xd7?? (9...♘xd7 10 ♘xd5 leaves White a pawn up) 10 ♗b5 because the a6-pawn is pinned against the rook on a8: 10...axb5 11 ♕xa8+ and White wins. The key line for our theme is **8...e6 9 g4! ♗g6 10 g5!**, forcing the knight to move from f6. This in turn leaves the knight on d7 without enough protection, and it is lost after **10...♘h5 11 ♘xd7**, since **11...♕xd7 12 ♗b5** costs Black his queen due to a *pin*.

TRAP 20   One-Two Punch by Pawn and Queen

You grab him, I'll smash him

Most opponents won't walk into a fork, but there are ways to lure them into one. For instance, a pawn might lay down its life with a decoy sacrifice so a queen check then wins a piece.

1 d4 ♘f6 2 ♗f4 c5 3 ♘f3?! cxd4. White has unwisely allowed his central pawn to be removed. Now 4 ♕xd4 ♘c6 gives Black excellent development, but after **4 ♘xd4?? e5!** things get much worse for White.

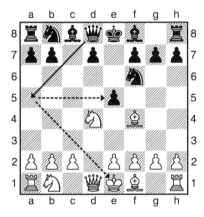

The pawn forks knight and bishop. But so what? White can just take it. **5 ♗xe5 ♕a5+**. This is the point: the pawn was a *decoy* to draw the bishop into a queen fork, and Black wins a piece.

After **1 d4 d5 2 ♘f3 ♗f5 3 c4 e6 4 g3 ♘f6 5 ♗g2 c5?! 6 cxd5 ♘xd5 7 0-0 ♗e7 8 dxc5** the position looks quiet, but White has seen a way for Black to go wrong! **8...♗xc5??** (8...0-0 is better, though after 9 ♘bd2 Black still needs to be careful as White is threatening the pawn fork e4) **9 e4!** Suddenly we have the first punch of our familiar pattern, even though the position looks very different. After **9...♗xe4 10 ♕a4+** Black can resign, as he is losing a bishop.

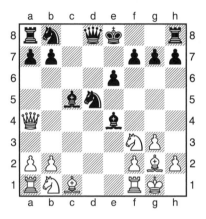

Next we have a more concealed version of the same idea, as it looks like White is developing very quietly. After **1 ♘f3 d5 2 g3 ♘f6 3 c4 ♗f5?!** (he should defend with 3...c6 or 3...e6, advance by 3...d4 or take with 3...dxc4) **4 cxd5** Black must waste time recapturing his pawn, as **4...♘xd5??** loses more than time!

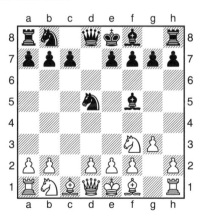

5 e4! ♗xe4 6 ♕a4+ wins a piece.

33

TRAP 21 Giving Up the Queen: Sting in the Tail

Doing the same thing and getting different results

Just because two positions look very similar, you can't assume that the same tactic will work in them both. In our first example, Black gives up his queen and wins it back with a ...♗b4+ idea, but in our second, the same trick falls flat on its face!

At a glance, **1 d4 ♘f6 2 c4 e6 3 ♘c3 d5 4 ♗g5 c5 5 ♘f3 cxd4 6 ♘xd4 e5 7 ♘db5?!** looks like a nice idea. The point is to meet **7...a6!** with **8 ♘xd5??**. However, this is a blunder, though a popular one: it has occurred in nearly half the games that have reached this position! If White sees the danger, he will probably find the forced move 8 ♕a4, though his game is still difficult after 8...♗d7. But what is the danger? After **8...axb5 9 ♘xf6+** it looks like White is winning. However...

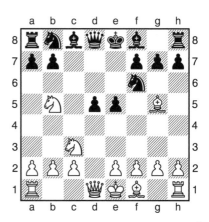

Now Black should play 6...d4 7 ♘d5! ♘a6!, where there is still everything to play for. After **6...a6??**, 7 ♘xd5! axb5 8 ♘xf6+ has won several games for White.

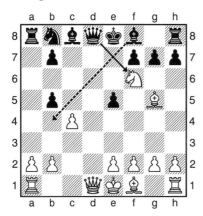

9...♕xf6! (not 9...gxf6??, when White wins by 10 ♕xd8+ ♔xd8 11 ♗xf6+ and ♗xh8) **10 ♗xf6 ♗b4+!**. Here is the sting in the tail! Black is a piece up after **11 ♕d2 ♗xd2+ 12 ♔xd2 gxf6**.

But be careful: often White's idea *does* work. **1 ♘c3 ♘f6 2 d4 c5 3 ♘f3 cxd4 4 ♘xd4 d5 5 ♗g5 e5 6 ♘db5** is completely different.

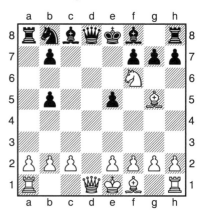

The fact that he has *not* played c4 means that after **8...♕xf6 9 ♗xf6 ♗b4+ 10 c3** the check is blocked and he keeps his extra queen.

34

TRAP 22 — Englund Trap and Relatives

"Look out for ...♕c1 mate" yelled the spectator

The Englund Gambit, **1 d4 e5?** is not a good opening, but it features one notable trap. The idea behind this trap is useful to know, as it can crop up in other situations.

After **2 dxe5 ♘c6 3 ♘f3 ♕e7 4 ♗f4 ♕b4+ 5 ♗d2 ♕xb2**, White should play 6 ♘c3!. But after **6 ♗c3?? ♗b4!** White is already lost.

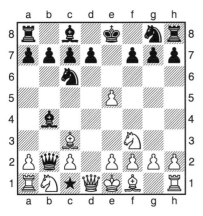

The key point is the surprising mate after **7 ♕d2 ♗xc3 8 ♕xc3 ♕c1#**.

Let's see some 'real' chess where the idea comes into play: **1 d4 ♘f6 2 ♘f3 c5 3 d5 b5 4 ♗g5 ♘e4 5 ♕d3 ♘xg5 6 ♘xg5 e6 7 ♘xf7**.

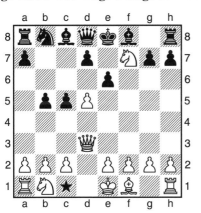

We shall see this theme in Trap 39, but Black has a good answer here. 7...♔xf7?! 8 dxe6+ ♔e7 9 ♘c3 is unsafe for Black, but after **7...♕f6! 8 ♘xh8 ♕xb2** we see the parallel with the Englund Gambit trap: **9 ♕c3??** is a blunder because of **9...♕c1#**. 9 e3 is best, with complex play ahead. The only way for White to try to save the rook is 9 c3? but 9...c4! 10 ♕d2 (or 10 ♕d1 b4!) 10...♕xa1 11 ♕c2 g6 intending ...♗g7 gives Black a superb position.

The black queen can suddenly land on c1 from another direction too: **1 d4 ♘f6 2 ♗g5 ♘e4 3 ♗h4 c5 4 ♕d3? ♕b6! 5 b3** (5 ♕xe4? ♕xb2 threatens mate and traps the rook) **5...♕h6!?** (the queen eyes both the c1-square and the loose bishop on h4).

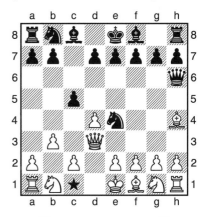

Now **6 ♕xe4?? walks into 6...♕c1#**, while 6 ♘f3 ♕c1+ 7 ♕d1 ♕b2 8 ♘bd2 ♘xd2 9 ♘xd2 ♕xd4 gives Black a useful extra pawn.

TRAP 23 | Smothered Mate: Not Always in the Corner

When a knight becomes a superhero

You are probably used to seeing smothered mates in the corner of the board. In the pattern known as Philidor's Legacy, a double check and a queen sacrifice force mate (we saw it in Trap 5). But smothered mates can occur in other places too, with or without sacrifices.

Let's start with a simple example. A top-class grandmaster (Reshevsky) was giving a simultaneous display and in a careless moment allowed an enemy knight to invade. **1 d4 ♘f6 2 c4 e6 3 ♘c3 ♗b4 4 e3 c5 5 ♘e2 d5 6 ♗d2 ♕a5?! 7 a3 ♘c6 8 axb4?**. Reshevsky assumes he is facing a very weak player who has simply blundered a piece – this happens a lot in simuls, of course. (Instead, 8 ♘g3 gives White an excellent game.) **8...♘xb4!**.

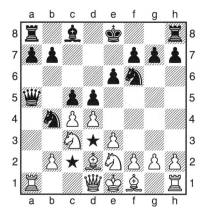

Oops! In the game, Reshevsky allowed the mate by **9 ♖xa5?? ♘d3#**, but he was already in a bad way. 9 ♘f4 allows the fork trick 9...♕xa1! 10 ♕xa1 ♘c2+ and 9 ♕a4+ ♕xa4 10 ♖xa4 ♘d3+ 11 ♔d1 ♘xf2+ 12 ♔c2 ♘xh1 costs him the rook in the other corner!

While strictly not a smothered mate, the following game, played in Germany, features several sacrifices to block flight-squares and set up a mate by a knight. **1 d4 d5 2 ♗f4 ♘f6 3 e3 c5 4 c3 ♘c6 5 ♘d2 ♗f5 6 ♘gf3 e6 7 ♗e2 cxd4 8 ♘xd4 ♗g6 9 ♗b5 ♕b6 10 a4 ♔d8?** (a terrible way to break the pin on the c6-knight! 10...a5 is safer) **11 a5** (11 ♘c4 ♕c5 12 ♘xc6+ bxc6 13 b4 is also winning, but we're mainly looking at this game for the beautiful mate that is soon to arise) **11...♘xa5 12 b4 ♘c6 13 ♘c4! dxc4 14 ♘xc6++ ♔c8 15 ♖xa7!**.

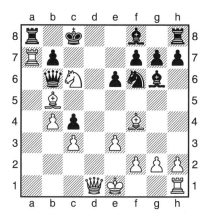

Now the actual game ended 15...♕xa7 16 ♕d8#, but the most amazing line is **15...♖xa7 16 ♕d8+! ♖xd8 17 ♘xa7#**. A whole queen down, White delivers a 'pure' mate with his three minor pieces!

Siberian Trap

From Russia with checkmate

This is an evil idea. A sudden knight leap overloads a key defender, allowing the queen to swoop in from far away and give a snap mate. The best-known version is in the Morra Gambit. But unlike most of the traps in the Morra, the Siberian Trap is sprung by *Black*.

It starts with **1 e4 c5 2 d4 cxd4 3 c3 dxc3 4 ♘xc3 ♘c6 5 ♘f3 e6 6 ♗c4 ♕c7** (or 6...♘f6 7 0-0 ♕c7) **7 0-0 ♘f6**. We start to see Black's idea after **8 ♕e2?! ♘g4!**. Now White is struggling to preserve any real compensation for the pawn he has gambited. Why? Black is threatening to win on the spot with 9...♘d4!, so White needs to play some defensive moves, rather than develop his initiative. In plenty of games, White has failed to see that Black can have threats of his own, with finishes like **9 h3?? ♘d4! 0-1**.

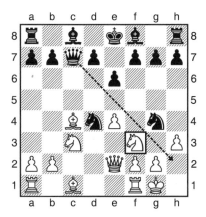

White either loses his queen or is mated by **10 ♘xd4** (10 ♕d3 solves nothing because of 10...♘xf3+ followed by 11...♕h2# after either recapture) **10...♕h2#**. In fact, the Siberian Trap is a risky line for Black because White should reply 8 ♘b5! ♕b8 9 e5! ♘g4 (9...♘xe5? 10 ♘xe5 ♕xe5 11 ♖e1 gives White an enormously strong attack;

9...a6 10 exf6 axb5 11 fxg7 ♗xg7 12 ♗xb5 is another possibility) 10 ♗f4.

OK, so the Morra is a 'speciality' line, and the Siberian Trap isn't the safest way to meet it. But the idea itself can be used in many other settings. It has claimed dozens of victims in the Queen's Gambit Accepted, in lines such as this: **1 d4 d5 2 ♘f3 ♘f6 3 c4 dxc4 4 e3 e6 5 ♗xc4 c5 6 0-0 a6 7 a4 ♘c6 8 ♕e2 ♕c7 9 ♘c3 ♗d6 10 dxc5 ♗xc5 11 e4?!**. White is trying to grab space and push Black's pieces back, but in fact he is just giving them good squares.

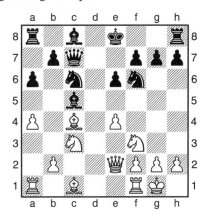

11...♘g4 (11...♘d4 is good too, but the move chosen sets a trap while preparing to grab central squares) **12 h3??** This blunder has been made, in this and similar positions, by a large number of players, even including masters. Of course, we already know what is wrong with it: **12...♘d4!** wins on the spot.

Invisible Double Attacks and Overloads

"How could I miss this move?"

Some tactics are not at all complex, but are easy to miss. This often happens if the move that allows them forms a logical part of a plan. Tactics trump logic!

After **1 e4 c5 2 ♘f3 d6 3 ♗c4 ♘f6 4 d3 ♘c6 5 c3**, **5...♗g4?** seems like a good and natural move: Black posts the bishop actively before developing with ...e6 and ...♗e7. However...

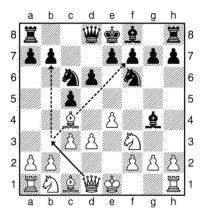

6 ♕b3! wins a pawn thanks to a simple double attack on b7 and f7. This little trick has caught more than 50 victims, and could have claimed more, as White has also missed the idea in several games, including ones with a strong grandmaster playing White!

In the next example, an innocent offer to exchange queens brings White's game to its knees. **1 d4 d5 2 ♘f3 ♘f6 3 c4 e6 4 g3 ♗b4+ 5 ♗d2 ♗e7 6 ♕b3 0-0 7 ♗g2 c6** and now **8 ♗b4?!** is an attempt to exchange off Black's 'good' bishop. There are three problems: it isn't yet clear which bishops will be 'good' and 'bad'; it costs time when there are still undeveloped pieces; *and* there is a specific

tactical problem. **8...dxc4! 9 ♕xc4?**. If White had realized the problem at this point, he would have played 9 ♗xe7 cxb3 10 ♗xd8 bxa2 11 ♗e7 axb1♕+ 12 ♖xb1, when he can hope for some compensation for the pawn.

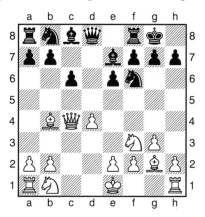

At first sight, **9...♕d5!** is an attempt to exchange queens. But in fact it creates a double attack in the form of an *overload* of the white queen. The key point is that after 10 ♕xd5? Black inserts 10...♗xb4+ before recapturing the queen. And after **10 ♕c3 ♘e4!** White has no good way to defend his bishop. **11 ♕a3?**. This obvious move loses on the spot. 11 ♗xe7 ♘xc3 12 ♘xc3 is essential, though Black is much better after 12...♕a5 13 ♗xf8 ♔xf8 – count the pieces! **11...♕c4!**. The final double attack is against the b4-bishop and a threat of mate on c1. This whole sequence has occurred in two games – in one of them a master had White.

Sicilian ♘db5 Trick: Disaster on d6

Burn one knight to open the door for its brother

In the Sicilian, a white knight suddenly landing on the d6-square can easily decide the game – even if White has to give up a whole piece to get it there.

A black knight on e7, boxing in the king, proves a problem here: **1 e4 c5 2 ♘f3 ♘c6 3 d4 cxd4 4 ♘xd4 e6 5 ♘c3 a6 6 a3 ♕c7 7 ♗e2 d6 8 0-0 ♘ge7??**. Black allows a standard trick that works in many such positions, if d6 is poorly covered and the queen is on c7.

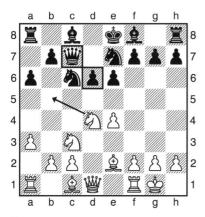

9 ♘db5!. One knight gives up its life so that its colleague can smash through on d6. **9...axb5 10 ♘xb5 ♕d8** (or 10...♕b6 11 ♘xd6+ ♔d7 12 ♗e3) **11 ♘xd6+** and Black loses his queen.

A similar idea can also work when the target is a bishop on d6. **1 e4 c5 2 ♘f3 ♘c6 3 d4 cxd4 4 ♘xd4 e6 5 ♘c3 a6 6 ♗e2 ♕c7 7 ♗e3 ♗d6 8 g3 ♘ge7**. Now the immediate 9 ♘db5 does not work because after 9...axb5 10 ♘xb5 Black has the saving check 10...♕a5+, when play might continue 11 ♗d2 ♗b4 12 c3 ♗c5 13 b4 ♘xb4 14 cxb4 ♗xb4 with a complicated game. So White calmly castles: **9 0-0**.

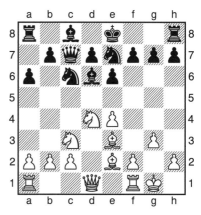

9...0-0??. Black follows suit, but does not realize that White has created a deadly threat. 9...♘xd4 is one safer option. **10 ♘db5! axb5 11 ♘xb5**. White has given up one knight, but will gain a bishop, keeping a good extra pawn. **11...♕a5 12 ♘xd6**.

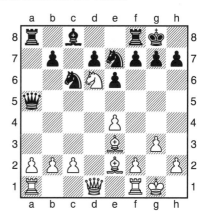

White will win easily. His pieces are well placed and Black's development is awful.

TRAP 27 — Castling Queenside with Check

When the king goes hunting for rooks

In very special situations, a king can win a rook that is three squares away! It sounds like black magic – let's see how it works.

1 d4 d5 2 c4 e6 3 ♘c3 c6 4 e4 ♗b4 5 ♗d3 e5 6 dxe5 dxe4 7 ♗xe4 ♗xc3+ 8 bxc3 ♕xd1+ 9 ♔xd1 ♗e6. White has won a pawn but has weak doubled isolated c-pawns. **10 ♖b1**. White seeks to go on the attack. **10...♘a6 11 ♖xb7??**. Grabbing a second pawn – what could possibly be wrong with that? Instead, 11 ♗e3 keeps Black under pressure.

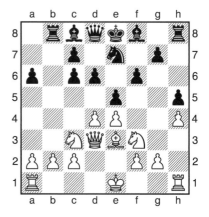

White prepares to castle while also setting the trap. **10...♖xb2?!** (risky, but not yet disastrous) **11 dxe5 dxe5??** (11...♘g6 allows Black to fight on; 11...fxe5? 12 ♘xe5! dxe5? 13 ♕xd8+ ♔xd8 14 0-0-0+ is White's main idea – he is the exchange up) **12 ♕xd8+ ♔xd8 13 0-0-0+**.

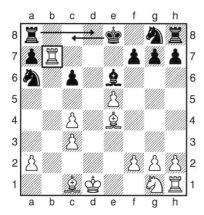

11...0-0-0+!. By castling queenside with check, Black wins a whole rook! (Remember the castling rules: it's only the king that can't move through check; it doesn't matter that the b8-square is attacked.)

Now that you have seen a simple form of this idea, it will be easier to understand a famous version. **1 e4 e5 2 ♘f3 ♘c6 3 ♗b5 a6 4 ♗a4 d6 5 ♗xc6+ bxc6 6 d4 f6 7 ♘c3 ♖b8**. Eyeing the b2-pawn, but we already know the potential problem. How to make it come true? **8 ♕d3 ♘e7 9 h4 h5 10 ♗e3**.

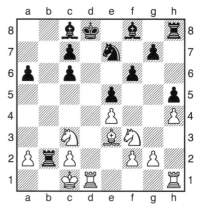

Castling with check wins the rook on b2.

TRAP 28 — Cambridge Springs Trap

A minor piece goes missing in small-town Pennsylvania

A number of traps in the Cambridge Springs Defence – **1 d4 d5 2 c4 e6 3 ♘c3 ♘f6 4 ♗g5 ♘bd7 5 e3 c6 6 ♘f3 ♕a5** – regularly claim victims up to good club-player level. There are two main themes: the obvious one is a pin on a white knight that can win a pawn if White isn't careful. The one that catches players unaware is a concealed attack on a white bishop on g5.

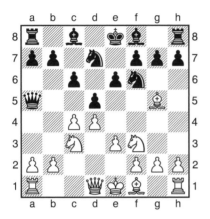

There are various pitfalls, but the most 'classic' is **7 ♘d2 ♗b4 8 ♕c2 0-0 9 ♗d3??**, when **9...dxc4** attacks two bishops at once.

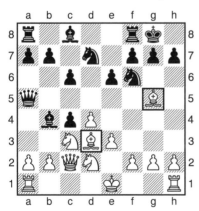

Sadly for White, **10 ♗xf6 cxd3** hits his queen. White's moves in this sequence look logical, but they fail for tactical reasons.

We can see that White might want to dodge the whole issue. But he could actually walk into something worse if he is not careful. Firstly, White can avoid putting his knight on c3: **1 d4 d5 2 c4 e6 3 ♘f3 ♘f6 4 ♗g5 ♘bd7 5 e3 c6 6 ♗d3 ♕a5+ 7 ♘bd2** (it is too late for 7 ♘c3?!, as this loses a pawn after 7...dxc4 8 ♗xc4 ♘e4) **7...dxc4 8 ♗xc4 ♘e4** and now White must make an important decision.

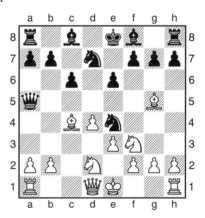

9 ♗h4?? loses to **9...g5! 10 ♗g3 g4** and, with ...♗b4 coming, White will lose his knight on d2. Surprisingly, 9 ♗f4! is much better, as after 9...g5?!, White is saved by 10 ♗c7!, *deflecting* the black queen.

White can also try putting his king's knight on e2, and we shall see a possible problem with that in the exercises at the end of the book!

41

Setting Up Knight Forks

Slot all the puzzle pieces into place

Of course, you can spot knight forks – but so can your opponents. So you may have to work a little to create a fork. Seek ways to sacrifice material in order to win back a larger amount with a knight fork. Let's see how the masters do it.

1 g3 g6 2 ♗g2 ♗g7 3 e4 c5 4 d3 ♘c6 5 c3. White prepares to play d4, but all pawn moves leave weak squares – in this case d3. **5...d6 6 ♗e3 ♕b6.** With this queen move, Black has seen the idea of a knight coming to d3 and forking e1 and b2. **7 ♕d2?!.** White should play 7 b3 and then get on with development. **7...♘e5!** creates a nasty threat, which White misses completely: **8 ♘a3??.** There's no ideal response, but after 8 b3 ♕a6 9 ♗f1 White isn't losing anything, even if he looks a bit silly.

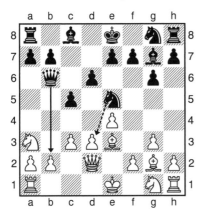

After **8...♕xb2!** White resigned in a game between two young Frenchmen. The queen attacks rook and knight, and 9 ♕xb2 ♘xd3+ followed by ...♘xb2 leaves White two pawns down and likely to lose a third on c3.

In the next example, a queen does even more work, provoking the key weakness and then exploiting it. **1 e4 c5 2 ♘c3 ♘c6 3 ♘f3 ♘f6 4 ♗b5 ♘d4 5 e5 ♘xb5 6 ♘xb5 ♘d5 7 ♘g5.** Believe it or not, this is a fairly popular opening line. With those active knights, expect fireworks! **7...f6 8 ♘e4 a6?!** (wasting time – Black should kick back the more central knight with 8...f5) **9 ♘bc3 ♘xc3 10 dxc3!.** White controls the centre and a lot of space. **10...d6? 11 exd6 exd6 12 ♗f4 d5?.** Black had no good way to defend the pawn, but now he is ripped apart.

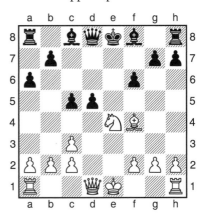

13 ♕h5+! g6 (13...♔e7 14 ♗d6+ is even worse) **14 ♕xd5!.** The point is **14...♕xd5 15 ♘xf6+** – a knight fork that two moves ago seemed unlikely as the f6-pawn was defended twice. White's queen check on h5 removed one defender, while the queen sacrifice removed the other one. White will be two pawns up with an easy endgame win ahead.

TRAP 30 — Bishop on e6 Provokes a Blunder

Peculiar does not mean bad

It's not clear why, but openings where Black puts a bishop in front of a pawn on the odd-looking square e6 seem to provoke an unusual number of blunders from White.

After **1 d4 d5 2 c4 dxc4 3 ♘f3 c6 4 e3**, the move **4...♗e6** looks very strange. The bishop will probably have to move again, but White may also have to waste time regaining the pawn on c4. However, in a shocking number of games White has decided to punish the 'silly' bishop move by immediately attacking it with his knight: **5 ♘g5??**.

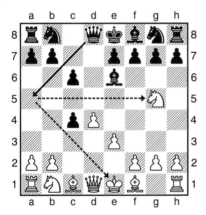

If the bishop now had to move, then White would have a great position. However, the queen fork **5...♕a5+!** wins the knight. This simple tactic has won a bunch of games, with masters and even grandmasters losing their knight. There must be something primitive-looking about the bishop on e6 that causes such strong players to lower their guard.

Similar blunders crop up in a number of openings. One in the Grünfeld has claimed some high-level victims. After **1 ♘f3 g6 2 d4 ♘f6 3 c4 ♗g7 4 ♘c3 d5 5 ♗g5 dxc4 6**
e3 ♗e6 the most common move is **7 ♘e5?**, but it shouldn't be! White wants to take the c4-pawn, but there is a problem. (7 ♗xc4?? is another example of our theme, losing to 7...♗xc4 8 ♕a4+ b5!.) **7...♘d5!**.

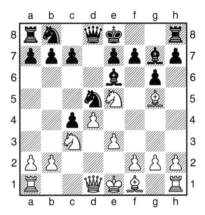

Black threatens a pawn fork with ...f6. **8 ♗xc4??** (8 ♘xc4 c5! gives Black a great game, but at least White isn't losing a piece) **8...♘xc3 9 bxc3 ♗xc4**. White is busted. Perhaps he had missed that 10 ♕a4+ fails because of 10...b5 – the bishop defends the pawn that rushes to its defence. The queen fork **10 ♘xc4 ♕d5** wins Black a piece, though he must be careful: 11 ♕g4 intends to mate Black on c8, but is parried with 11...f5. 11 ♘e5 allows the double attack 11...♗xe5! 12 dxe5 ♕xg2.

The moral is clear: don't be distracted by a move's odd appearance, but choose your moves based on what the move does. Beware of routine thinking!

TRAP 31   Overshot Bishop Perils

Unconventional development? Check the tactics radar

A fianchetto is a standard way to develop a bishop: a knight's pawn advances one square and the bishop moves behind it. But players might see a good reason to slide the bishop one square further, to the edge of the board. Perhaps the bishop attacks a pawn, or prepares to exchange off an enemy piece. However, this also leaves the bishop more exposed.

1 d4 ♘f6 2 c4 e6 3 ♘c3 ♗b4 4 e3 b6 5 ♘e2 ♗a6 6 ♘g3 d5??. This blunder has been played a number of times, and even by a grandmaster. Black normally chooses 6...♗xc3+ 7 bxc3 d5 or plays 6...0-0 before deciding whether to go for ...d5, and White's next move explains why.

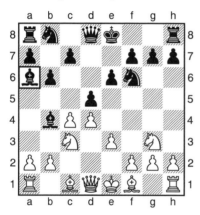

7 ♕a4+!. If Black's bishop were back on the more conventional square b7, he would be able to defend the b4-bishop by playing ...♘c6. But with it more aggressively placed on a6, he simply loses a piece.

The overshot bishop might also allow the rook in the corner to come under attack – like in the *Uncompleted Fianchetto* (Trap 72). **1 d4 ♘f6 2 c4 e6 3 ♘f3 b6 4 a3 ♗a6** (4...♗b7 is a standard fianchetto, but putting the bishop on a6 annoys White by attacking the c4-pawn) **5 ♕c2**. Both sides' play may look odd if you have only studied basic

'rules of development', but the moves have a solid logic, and have been used many times by grandmasters. **5...c5 6 d5 exd5 7 cxd5 ♘xd5??**. But this move is definitely not OK – the d5-pawn was not a free gift! **8 ♕e4+**.

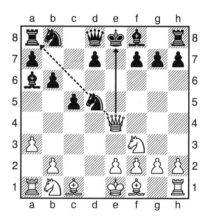

If the bishop were on b7 instead of a6, then this queen check would be pointless. As things stand, it wins a piece. **8...♘e7**. The knight saves its own skin, but exposes a more valuable piece in the corner. **9 ♕xa8 ♘ec6**. Black hopes to trap the white queen, but it will be a fruitless effort. At worst, White will get two rooks for the queen – a small material gain – but a little calculation shows he can do far better. 10 ♘e5 ♘xe5 11 ♕e4 is an 'emergency exit', while the greedier **10 e3! b5 11 a4 ♕c8 12 axb5 ♗b7 13 ♕xb7 ♕xb7 14 bxc6** is even worse for Black.

TRAP 32

More Queen Forks

The perfect weapon against widely scattered targets

The knight is famous for its forking ability, but the queen is the piece most capable of attacking many pieces at the same time. If there are loose enemy pieces, chances are the queen can find a way to attack them.

The ultra-short game **1 d4 ♞f6 2 ♗g5 c6 3 e3?? ♛a5+ 0-1** shows one of the earliest queen forks. Black wins the bishop for nothing. White's 3 e3?? blunder has even been played by masters, and I understand how. White wants to keep his options open. Taking on f6 or moving a knight makes it easier for Black to choose a plan. 3 e3 is a way to keep him guessing. Unfortunately it loses a piece!

Now let's look at the queen forking two minor pieces. **1 d4 ♞f6 2 c4 c5 3 d5 b5 4 cxb5 a6 5 bxa6 g6 6 g3 ♗g7 7 ♗g2 d6 8 ♞c3 0-0 9 ♞f3 ♗xa6 10 0-0 ♞bd7 11 ♖e1 ♞g4 12 ♛c2 ♖b8??.**

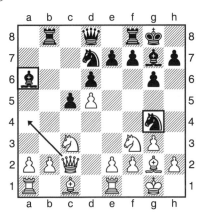

This position has occurred in a number of games, but in only one of them has White played the simple queen fork **13 ♛a4!**, winning a piece. How can this one-move tactic be so hard (for both players) to see? Perhaps it is because White's queen has just moved

from d1 to c2: immediately continuing on to a4 is not a move we tend to consider. Black's 12...♖b8?? is a type of blunder we see many times throughout this book: White had no particular threat, so Black casually plays a 'useful' move, assuming there is still no danger.

The next example is more sophisticated. White puts a similar tactic to work to win a pawn, rather than a piece. **1 d4 ♞f6 2 c4 e6 3 ♞f3 b6 4 a3 c5 5 d5 ♗a6 6 ♛c2 exd5 7 cxd5 g6 8 ♞c3 ♗g7 9 g3 0-0 10 ♗g2 d6 11 0-0 ♞bd7 12 ♗f4 ♛e7 13 ♖fe1 ♞g4?!.**

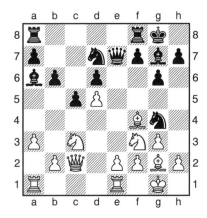

Black wants to put a knight on the excellent central square e5, but there is a problem, as White can target a6 and g4: **14 ♛a4! ♗b7 15 ♗xd6** (discovering an attack on the g4-knight) **15...♛xd6 16 ♛xg4** and White has won a pawn. This has been played twice at grandmaster level, and while Black has some play for the pawn, he has lost both times.

TRAP 33   Pin on the e-File Wins a Pawn

"See a pawn and pick it up; Drop it in his coffee cup" – Bill Hartston

This idea is simple but very effective. The typical set-up is: White takes a pawn on e5 with his knight. Black recaptures with a knight or bishop. Then a white rook comes to e1, pinning the black piece against its king, winning it and keeping the extra pawn. I used this idea myself to win a key game on the way to winning my first junior championship.

1 g3 d5 2 ♘f3 c5 3 ♗g2 ♘c6 4 0-0 e5 5 d3 f5?! 6 c4 d4 7 e3 ♘f6 8 exd4 cxd4?. This position has occurred in a number of games, and is very common with reversed colours. However, with Black a move behind in his development, his king is exposed on the e-file, which allows our tactic:

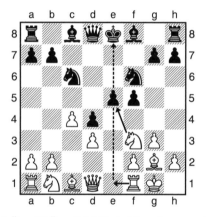

9 ♘xe5! ♘xe5 10 ♖e1. There's no saving the knight, as White can easily attack e5 again with bishop and pawn: **10...♘g4 11 f4** (White has several other excellent options, but this is simple and good) **11...♗b4 12 ♖e2** and fxe5 leaves White a pawn up.

It is quite common to need to use the f-pawn to win the pinned piece: **1 e4 c6 2 d4 d5 3 ♘d2 g6 4 ♘gf3 ♘h6 5 h3 ♗g7 6 ♗d3 f6 7 0-0 e5?** (Black fights for the centre before he has developed enough pieces to back up this aggressive play).

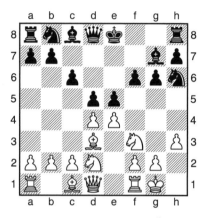

8 exd5 cxd5 9 dxe5 fxe5 10 ♘xe5! ♗xe5 11 ♖e1 ♘c6 12 ♘f3 ♘f7 13 ♘xe5 (or 13 ♗b5, removing a defender) **13...♘fxe5 14 f4.**

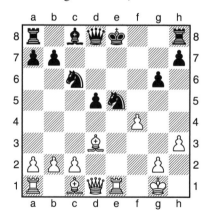

White makes sure of regaining his piece. After **14...0-0 15 fxe5** White is a good pawn up and should go on to win.

The ♘xe5 and ♗b5+ Queen Sacrifice

A standard punishment for an over-optimistic pin

This unpinning queen sacrifice is very common and has led to many quick victories. It happens when a knight on f3 captures on e5, allowing a black bishop to take the queen on d1. Then comes a powerful bishop check on b5. Sometimes this wins on the spot; other times it wins after some complex tactics. Sometimes it is just unclear or it fails completely. Let's see some examples.

1 ♘f3 d5 2 c4 ♘f6?! 3 cxd5 ♘xd5 4 e4 ♘f6 5 ♘c3 ♘c6?! 6 d4 ♗g4? 7 d5. Black has played the opening badly, and White has seized full control of the centre. With **7...♘e5?** Black tries to exploit a pin, but White has a deadly reply: **8 ♘xe5! ♗xd1 9 ♗b5+**. Here is the key bishop check, but Black can interpose a pawn. Has White miscalculated? **9...c6 10 dxc6!**.

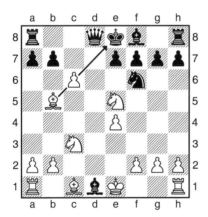

No, because this white pawn now becomes a monster, with threats of discovered check and promotion. 10...♕c7 blocks the pawn's advance to c7 but allows 11 cxb7+ and bxa8♕+. 10...bxc6 11 ♗xc6+ ♘d7 12 ♗xd7+ costs Black his queen. **10...a6** looks toughest, but allows the pawn to take the

black queen itself: **11 c7+! axb5 12 cxd8♕+ ♖xd8 13 ♘xd1** and White has a whole piece more.

Here the theme occurred in more concealed but equally devastating form: **1 d4 d5 2 ♗g5 ♘f6 3 ♘d2 ♗f5 4 c4 e6 5 ♘gf3 ♘bd7 6 ♘h4 ♗e4 7 cxd5 exd5** and now **8 ♘xe4??** looks like a simple exchange of pieces but is actually a fatal mistake.

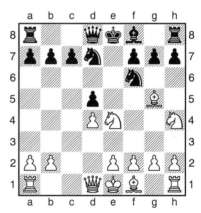

8...♘xe4! 9 ♗xd8 (9 ♗d2 would safely cover the weak e1-a5 diagonal except for the *loose knight* on h4, so 9...♕xh4 wins; 9 ♘f3 ♘xg5 also costs White a piece) **9...♗b4+ 10 ♕d2 ♗xd2+ 11 ♔d1 ♖xd8** and Black is a piece up. This all happened 90 years ago in a British championship game.

TRAP 35 — Sicilian Pin-Breaking

A solid reward for careful calculation

This idea can arise in many openings, but is most common in the Sicilian Defence. A knight on f6 has been pinned by a bishop on g5. Against all odds, the knight takes a white pawn on e4, even though it looks very well-defended.

1 e4 c5 2 ♘f3 ♘c6 3 d4 cxd4 4 ♘xd4 ♘f6 5 ♘c3 e5 6 ♘db5 d6 7 ♗g5 a6 8 ♘a3 ♗e6 9 ♘c4 ♖c8 10 ♘e3 ♗e7. It seems Black is simply developing his pieces, but he has just set up for a typical trick. White must choose his next move carefully, but many players are unaware of the danger. **11 ♗d3?**. White has everything doubly covered, but in fact it all comes crashing down right away. 11 ♗e2 0-0 12 0-0? ♘xe4! is another form of the trick.

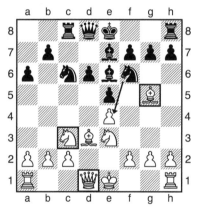

11...♘xe4!. Here it is: the Sicilian Unpin. It looks like magic, but the logic is solid. Now 12 ♗xe4 and 12 ♘xe4 are both answered with 12...♗xg5. The key point is that after **12 ♗xe7** Black inserts **12...♘xc3** before taking the bishop on e7. This attacks the white queen, so White can *exchange* queens if he wishes, but is not *winning* one! After both 13 bxc3 ♕xe7 and 13 ♗xd8 ♘xd1 14 ♖xd1 ♖xd8 Black is a very good pawn up.

The unpin doesn't always succeed. The knight must attack the white queen when it lands on c3, and threats to the black king can ruin everything too. Also, there are lines where the knight gets trapped, such as **1 e4 c5 2 ♘f3 d6 3 d4 cxd4 4 ♘xd4 ♘f6 5 ♘c3 a6 6 ♗c4 e6 7 ♗g5 ♗e7 8 ♗b3 ♘xe4??**.

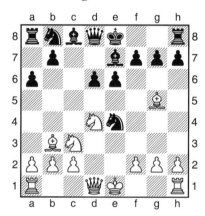

This would work with the bishop on e2, but on b3 it protects a4 and c4, which makes a huge difference. **9 ♗xe7! ♘xc3 10 ♗xd8 ♘xd1 11 ♗c7** leaves the knight trapped. After **11...♘xb2 12 ♖b1** it has no escape.

When I started playing competitive chess, this ...♘xe4 possibility seemed to come up in a lot of my games. I recall it always being hard work to analyse the long sequences of captures and figure out what was going on at the end of them. I wish I could give simple rules of thumb, but there is no substitute for carefully working it out move by move.

TRAP 36   Sicilian Unpin: Advanced Forms

It works outside Sicily too!

Now we'll look at a couple of deeper examples based on the Sicilian Unpin. Actually, neither of them comes from a Sicilian Defence at all, which goes to show how chess ideas can be transplanted from one opening to another.

1 e4 e5 2 ♗c4 d6 3 ♘c3 ♘f6 4 d3 ♗e6 5 ♗g5 ♗e7 6 ♘ge2?! ♗xc4!. Black spots a hidden problem with White's set-up. **7 dxc4?** (White should bail out with 7 ♗xf6 ♗xf6 8 dxc4) **7...♘xe4!**.

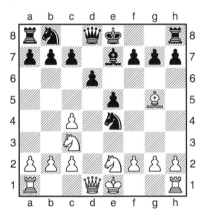

Here is the familiar Unpin, in an unfamiliar setting! And it works perfectly. **8 ♗xe7** (8 ♘xe4 ♗xg5 gives Black an extra pawn – same as usual) **8...♘xc3 9 ♗xd8** (or 9 ♘xc3 ♕xe7) **9...♘xd1**. We have the usual calculation chore... **10 ♗xc7 ♘xb2 11 c5!?** (11 ♗xd6 ♘xc4 just happens to defend e5 while attacking the bishop) **11...♘c4 12 0-0-0 ♘a6 13 ♗xd6 ♖c8**. Although Black isn't a pawn up at the moment, he has an excellent position and much better pawns, and went on to win in the Hungarian game that we have been following.

The next example comes from Philidor's Defence. **1 e4 d6 2 d4 ♘f6 3 ♘c3 e5 4 ♘f3**

exd4 5 ♕xd4 a6 6 ♗g5 ♗e7 7 h3 ♘c6 8 ♕d2 ♗e6 9 ♘d4 ♘xd4 10 ♕xd4 0-0 11 ♗e2 ♖e8 12 0-0?.

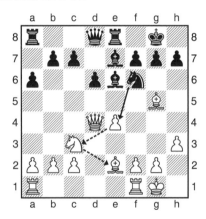

So what can this position possibly have to do with our theme? It is certainly not a Sicilian, and the white queen is on d4 (rather than d1 or e2). But tactics have a way of exploiting any looseness in a position... **12...♘xe4! 13 ♕xe4**. The key point is that after 13 ♗xe7 ♘xc3 Black threatens to fork the white king and queen by taking the bishop on e2, so 14 ♗xd8?? (14 ♕xc3 ♕xe7 gives Black a solid extra pawn) 14...♘xe2+ 15 ♔h1 ♘xd4 leaves White a piece down. **13...♗xg5 14 ♕xb7 ♖b8 15 ♕xa6 ♖xb2** and although White has clawed back his pawn, all Black's pieces are very active and White's pawns are broken. We have been viewing a game from France, and Black went on to win this one too.

TRAP 37

♘d5: Queen vs Queen

When two queens go to war, a point is all that you can score

Again our theme is most important in the Sicilian Defence, but can occur in almost any opening. All it needs is a white queen on d2, a black queen on a5, and a white knight on c3. Playing ♘d5 uncovers an attack on the black queen. This can lead to an exchange of queens, but sometimes wins a pawn, or much more...

1 d4 ♘f6 2 ♗g5 ♘e4 3 ♗f4 c5 4 f3 ♘f6 5 dxc5 ♘a6 6 e4 ♘xc5 7 ♘c3 d6 8 ♕d2 ♗d7 9 0-0-0 ♕a5 10 ♔b1. This sneaky sidestep by the king is often a key move to set up the ♘d5 theme. The king protects the a2-pawn and now an exchange of queens on d2 will not come with check. **10...♖d8??**. Not seeing the danger, Black makes things far worse. 10...♖c8 is better. 10...g6 is an obvious move, but White can use our theme to weaken Black's pawns: 11 ♘d5 ♕xd2 12 ♘xf6+ exf6 13 ♖xd2 leaves the d6-pawn open to attack.

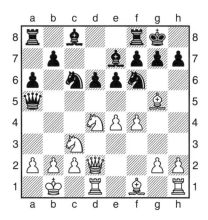

After **11 ♘xc6! bxc6 12 ♘d5!** Black loses material: 12...♕d8 13 ♘xe7+ ♕xe7 and 14 e5 wins a piece thanks to the pin. After 12...♕xd2 it is vital that 13 ♘xe7+ is check. **12...♗d8** desperately tries to hang on.

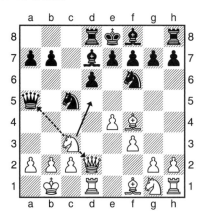

11 ♘d5! ♕xd2 (otherwise Black loses his queen) **12 ♘c7#**. Thanks to the rook being on d8, it's smothered mate!

Here is a more typical case in the Sicilian: **1 e4 c5 2 ♘f3 ♘c6 3 d4 cxd4 4 ♘xd4 ♘f6 5 ♘c3 d6 6 ♗g5 e6 7 ♕d2 ♗e7 8 0-0-0 0-0 9 f4 a6 10 ♔b1 ♕a5??**.

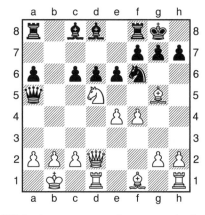

White has many good answers, including **13 ♘e7+! ♔h8 14 ♕xd6** threatening ♘g6+.

50

Rampant Pawns and the Long Diagonal

It cannot be reasoned with...

Have you never seen a pawn run amok? At a speed of one square at a time, it seems unlikely. But when it uncovers an attack from another piece, it gains time to cause havoc in the enemy camp. Here we see the pawn opening up an attack on the long diagonal, allowing an exchange of bishops. But we don't recapture the bishop! Instead the pawn eats more enemy pieces.

Let's start with a clear-cut example. **1 ♘f3 ♘f6 2 c4 e6 3 g3 b6 4 ♗g2 ♗b7 5 0-0 c5 6 ♘c3 ♗e7 7 ♖e1 d6 8 e4 ♘bd7 9 d4 cxd4 10 ♘xd4**. This is a well-known opening called the Hedgehog. Now Black normally plays 10...♕c7, but it is easy to miss that White has a threat. **10...a6??** is a very common blunder, played in dozens of games.

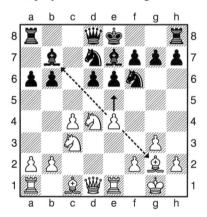

After the advance **11 e5!** White wins material. **11...♗xg2 12 exf6!** is the key point: two black pieces are attacked and he must lose one of them. 11...dxe5 is the only way to play on, but after 12 ♗xb7 exd4 13 ♗xa8 dxc3 14 ♗g2 White should win.

But when the bishop lands on g2, what if it is attacking a rook on f1? Then careful calculation is needed. **1 c4 c5 2 ♘c3 b6 3 g3 ♗b7 4 e4 e6 5 ♗g2 ♘f6 6 ♘ge2 ♗e7 7 0-0 d6?**. Either Black misses that the pawn can

go rampant, or thinks it doesn't work. **8 e5! ♗xg2 9 exf6 ♗xf1**. The bishop has a whole row of pieces to take, but so has the pawn! After **10 fxe7** Black sadly realizes that he has been tricked.

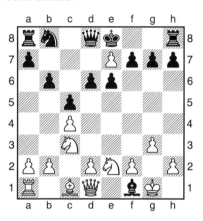

10...♗xe2? attacks the white queen, but it doesn't matter as 11 exd8♕+ comes *with check*. So the white pawn wins the eating contest! After **10...♕xe7 11 ♕xf1** White has ♗+♘ for ♖+♙ – a useful material advantage, and White has won all the games that have reached this position.

This idea is easy to miss – perhaps because we assume that a captured piece will be recaptured. It continues to appear in master-level games, and even in an important blitz game between Carlsen and Caruana – the two players in the 2018 world championship match!

TRAP 39   ♘xf7: More Rampant Pawns

Greasing the pawn's path forward

We have just seen how a pawn can become turbocharged when it uncovers an attack on the long diagonal. Here we have a similar set-up, but first a knight is sacrificed on f7 to draw the black king to that square. Then the pawn capture dxe6 comes with check, and the white bishop from g2 can take the black bishop on b7, winning material.

We start with a basic example. **1 d4 e6 2 ♘f3 f5 3 g3 b6 4 d5!? ♗e7 5 ♗g2 ♗b7 6 ♘e5**. White sets up the threat. The only thing that makes it hard to see is that the knight sacrifice will be on an empty square. Generally players expect sacrifices to come with a capture or at least a check, so this is a common blindspot. **6...d6?? 7 ♘f7!**.

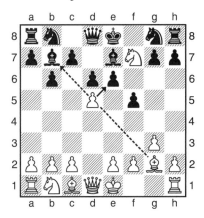

Perfectly demonstrating the theme. After **7...♔xf7 8 dxe6+** followed by **♗xb7**, White wins at least a piece. 7...♕c8 8 ♘xh8 e5 9 e4 happened in a student event in the 1950s, and Black decided to resign at this point.

Normally a little more setting-up is needed to lure an alert opponent into this type of trap. **1 d4 d5 2 c4 e6 3 ♘f3 a6 4 g3 dxc4 5 ♗g2 b5 6 ♘e5 ♖a7** (Black needs to be very careful once he has put his rook on this awkward square) **7 ♗e3 ♗b7?** (7...f6 is good).

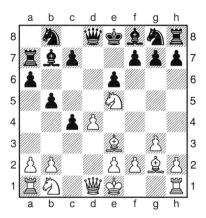

8 d5! (White finds a way to engineer the ♘xf7 idea) **8...♖a8 9 ♘xf7!** (our previous theme, 9 dxe6? ♕xd1+ 10 ♔xd1 ♗xg2 11 exf7+, offers White little good here).

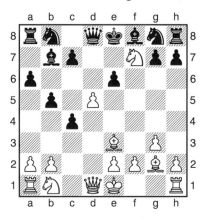

It's a knockout. After **9...♔xf7 10 dxe6+** and ♗xb7, the rook is trapped in the corner.

52

Dastardly a-Pawn Discoveries

Loose Rooks Drop Off!

When we imagine discovered attacks, we tend to think of moves by knights and bishops. But even the humblest of pawns can execute a deadly discovered attack. It is especially unexpected when it comes from a rook's pawn making a capture.

One of the simplest examples is in the Grünfeld Defence: **1 d4 ♘f6 2 c4 g6 3 ♘c3 d5 4 ♘f3 ♗g7 5 ♕b3 dxc4 6 ♕xc4 0-0 7 e4 a6**. Black plans to play ...b5, gaining space on the queenside. **8 a4?** seems like a natural way to prevent this idea, but it fails completely. In fact, it makes Black's plan far stronger! **8...b5!** comes with great force.

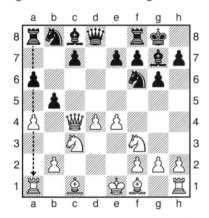

That's because **9 axb5??** (after 9 ♕b3 c5! Black launches an all-out assault on White's centre, and White's pawn on a4 becomes irrelevant) **9...axb5** attacks the white queen and rook, winning on the spot.

Sometimes the discovered attack works even as a rook sacrifice, thanks to a queentrap theme: **1 ♘f3 d5 2 g3 ♘f6 3 ♗g2 g6 4 0-0 ♗g7 5 c4 d4 6 e3 c5 7 exd4 cxd4 8 d3 ♘c6 9 ♕a4**. The queen intends to support a pawn advance, but after **9...0-0 10 b4 ♘d7 11 ♘bd2? a5!** White has no good reply.

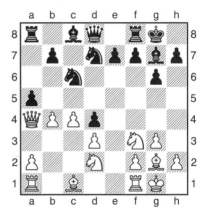

Now 12 b5 ♘c5 gives the black knights superb squares. He might try to avoid this with **12 ♗a3??**, controlling c5 before moving his b-pawn. But there is a huge tactical problem: **12...axb4!**. The discovery works even though the rook is undefended here! After **13 ♕xa8 ♘b6** the queen is trapped.

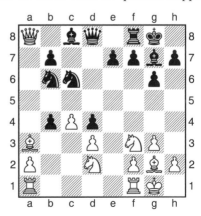

TRAP 41   Minor Piece Trapped by Pawns

Different traps for different folks

Both bishops and knights can be trapped by pawns, but the methods are different for each piece.

To run a knight out of squares, enemy pawns need to cover a few scattered squares, and for 'friendly' pieces to block the knight's retreat-squares. A knight on the edge is easier to trap than one in the centre. Here is a simple example. **1 e4 g6 2 d4 ♗g7 3 ♘f3 d6 4 c3 ♘f6 5 ♗d3 0-0 6 0-0 c5 7 h3 ♘c6 8 d5 ♘a5**.

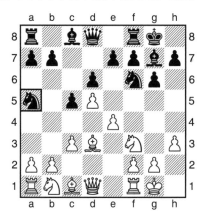

Black hopes that this knight will be useful on the queenside, but care is needed. For now the knight is safe because 9 b4?! allows 9...cxb4 10 cxb4 ♘d7, spearing the rook in the corner. So after White continued developing with **9 ♖e1** you should understand why **9...e5??** was a horrible mistake. With **10 b4!** White simply traps the knight – now there are no tricks and the knight will be captured. This actually happened in a game between supergrandmasters, played at a rapid time-limit.

To trap a bishop, the pawns need to control a number of squares on a diagonal, and for the bishop's retreat to be blocked off.

Here is a sophisticated trap in the English Opening that keeps claiming victims: **1 c4 e5 2 g3 ♘f6 3 ♗g2 d5 4 cxd5 ♘xd5 5 ♘c3 ♘b6 6 ♘f3 ♘c6 7 0-0 ♗e7 8 a3 ♗e6 9 d3 f6 10 b4 a5 11 b5 ♘d4 12 ♘d2**. Both sides have played logically. The queenside pawns can be arranged slightly differently and the trap still works, but the white pawn does need to be on b5 – *try to work out why on your own*. **12...♘d5??** Black thinks he has seized the initiative, but his pieces are about to run out of squares.

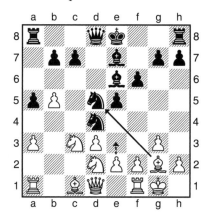

13 ♗xd5! is an easy move to overlook – in many games White has missed his chance too! You'd normally not exchange a fianchettoed bishop for a knight, as it leaves the king weak. But if it wins a piece... **13...♗xd5 14 e3**. Amazingly, Black must lose one of his two 'beautifully' centralized pieces! 14...♘f5 15 e4 forks the two pieces, while 14...♘e6 leaves the bishop high and dry on d5, so 15 e4 traps it mid-board.

TRAP 42

A Not-So-Loose Pawn

Tempting queens to their doom for 400 years

Sometimes we can effectively defend a pawn without tying up a piece protecting it directly – instead we use a little piece of tactics. The idea we are about to examine is nothing new – it was even mentioned in Greco's famous manuscript from around 1620 – but keeps claiming victims.

1 e4 d5 2 exd5 ♕xd5 3 ♘c3 ♕d6 4 d4 ♘f6 5 g3 c6 6 ♗f4 ♕b4?!. Black perhaps imagines that with the attack on b2 he has taken charge of the game. But White has an excellent reply. 6...♕d8 is preferable. **7 a3!**. Now Black cannot take on b2, and must spend more time with his queen. (7 ♖b1 defends the pawn directly, but allows Black to develop actively with 7...♗g4 or 7...♗f5.)

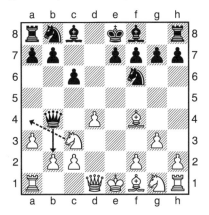

If Black does now take the pawn with **7...♕xb2??** (as some players have done), he will be shocked to find that **8 ♘a4** traps and wins the queen. Every square is covered!

This neat way to defend the b2-pawn can be used in many situations. As long as the knight is ready to come to a4 and trap the queen, the pawn is safe. Here is a more complex example, which has ensnared some strong players, including a grandmaster. **1 e4 d6 2 d4 ♘f6 3 ♘c3 c6 4 f4 ♕a5 5 ♗d3 e5 6 ♘f3 ♗g4 7 ♗e3 exf4 8 ♗xf4 ♕b6**. White now has a number of good moves, including 9 ♕d2 ♗xf3 10 gxf3 ♕xd4 11 0-0-0, with great play for the pawn, or our theme move 9 a3. But let's look at **9 ♘a4 ♕a5+ 10 ♘c3 ♕b4?!**. Black might believe that he is forcing the pace, but in fact he is edging towards the abyss. He should go back (with 10...♕b6). **11 a3! ♕xb2?? 12 ♘a4 ♗xf3 13 gxf3** and Black has resigned around here in a number of games.

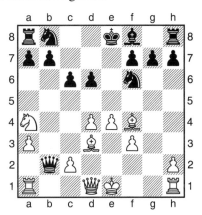

Is the queen really trapped? Yes, because **13...♕xd4 14 c3!** provides the final piece of the puzzle.

TRAP 43   More Queen Traps: Cornered!

That ain't no place for a lady

Even the mighty queen's mobility is reduced in the corners of the board, so here it is most in danger of being trapped. After a raid by the queen to grab a rook, check if it can escape.

1 e4 c5 2 ♘f3 ♘c6 3 ♗b5 g6 4 0-0 ♗g7 5 c3 ♘f6 6 e5 ♘d5 7 d4 cxd4 8 cxd4 0-0 9 ♗g5 ♕b6?!. Black targets b2, but White has a good answer: **10 ♗c4!**. Now **10...♕xb2??** is consistent but disastrous.

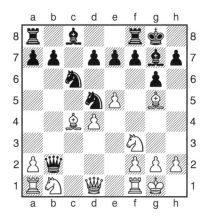

11 ♗xd5 ♕xa1. Black has won a rook for a knight, but not checked that his queen has an exit. **12 ♕d2!** wins.

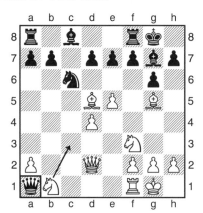

White covers the b2-square, so ♘c3 will win the black queen. This was a rapidplay game between two supergrandmasters, Judit Polgar and Joël Lautier.

In the next example, Black plays a little combination, but it fails because the queen never gets back alive after its raid of the white queenside. **1 e4 e6 2 d4 d5 3 ♘c3 ♗b4 4 e5 c5 5 a3 ♗xc3+ 6 bxc3 ♕c7 7 ♘f3 ♘c6 8 ♗d3 cxd4?!**. Black opens the game and 'undoubles' White's pawns. As White has more active pieces, this doesn't make sense unless there is a strong follow-up. Black has an idea in mind, but it doesn't work. **9 cxd4 ♘xd4??**.

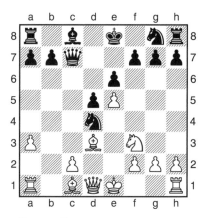

10 ♘xd4 ♕c3+ is the point: the queen forks three white pieces. But after the accurate reply **11 ♕d2!**, both captures cost Black his queen. 11...♕xd4 is answered with the discovered attack 12 ♗b5+!, while after **11...♕xa1, 12 c3!** and ♘b3 wins the queen.

Plenty of places to run, but nowhere to hide

Thanks to its power to move freely in all directions, a queen in the centre of the board can usually escape attacks with great ease. But not always!

1 e4 e5 2 ♘f3 ♘c6 3 ♗c4 ♗c5 4 0-0 ♘f6 5 d4 exd4 (1 e4 e5 2 ♘f3 ♘c6 3 ♗c4 ♘f6 4 d4 exd4 5 0-0 ♗c5 is another path to the same position) **6 e5 d5 7 exf6 dxc4** is a crazy sequence known as the Max Lange Attack. Both sides can avoid it if they wish to, but it leads to exciting chess. Here we see a way for Black to centralize his queen beautifully... only to get it trapped! **8 ♖e1+ ♗e6 9 fxg7 ♖g8 10 ♗g5 ♕d5??**. It is hard to believe this is a losing move. (10...♗e7 is best.) With **11 ♘c3!** White exploits two pins. **11...♕f5** (11...♕d7 12 ♘e4 ♗e7 13 ♘f6+ ♗xf6 14 ♗xf6 is also terrible for Black) **12 ♘e4!**.

traps the queen, since a knight check on f6 will win it if it moves to any of the squares that aren't attacked directly.

Our second queen trap arises in another traditional opening: the Two Knights Defence. **1 e4 e5 2 ♘f3 ♘c6 3 ♗c4 ♘f6 4 ♘g5 d5 5 exd5 ♘a5 6 ♗b5+ c6 7 dxc6 bxc6 8 ♗e2 h6 9 ♘f3 e4 10 ♘e5**. Black has sacrificed a pawn in return for easy development and space. There is no need for him to panic and try to force any immediate gains. So **10...♕d4?!** is the wrong idea.

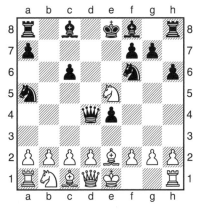

After **11 f4 ♗c5 12 ♖f1** Black's crude mate threat has been stopped, and White will force him back with moves like d3 and c3. But only the final attempt to force the pace with **12...♘d5??** leads to disaster, as **13 c3** unexpectedly traps the queen in the very middle of the board.

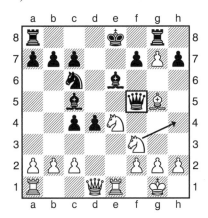

With **12...♖xg7** Black removes the 'potential queen', but loses the actual one! (12...♗e7 13 ♗xe7 followed by ♘xd4 also leaves Black in deep trouble.) Then **13 ♘h4**

TRAP 45 — The Grandmaster's Queen Trap

Your bishops can win Dad's queen too!

This idea works against players of all levels, but I was shocked to see how many high-ranked players have lost their queen this way. The pattern is not complex: two bishops (together with some pawns) cover all of a queen's possible squares. So why is it easily missed? Because it looks like there is a 'loophole' allowing the queen to escape, but this is cruelly denied with a surprising move by the enemy queen. We start with a basic example.

1 e4 e6 2 d4 d5 3 ♘d2 dxe4 4 ♘xe4 ♗d7 5 ♘f3 ♗c6 6 ♗d3 ♘f6 7 ♘xf6+ ♕xf6??. Black's play looks natural, yet after just seven moves he is dead lost. (7...gxf6 is essential.) After **8 ♗g5!** the black queen has no escape-squares, but has White overlooked Black's next move? **8...♗xf3** strips the defender away from the g5-bishop and attacks the white queen. But it doesn't help after **9 ♕d2!**.

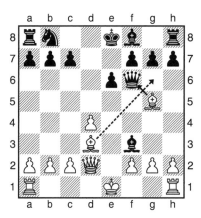

The queen sidesteps and supports the g5-bishop. The final point is **9...♕xd4 10 ♗b5+!**, a deadly discovered attack on the black queen. This pattern has been used to win dozens of games. But always check if Black's 'loophole' works – in some positions White must choose a different square for his queen (*hint:* that may come up in the exercises at the end of the book).

Now let's see a more intricate example on the same theme but with added checkmate motifs. **1 e4 e6 2 d4 d5 3 ♘d2 dxe4 4 ♘xe4 ♘f6 5 ♘xf6+ ♕xf6 6 ♘f3 h6 7 ♗d3 ♗d6 8 0-0** (8 ♕e2 0-0? 9 ♕e4! is similar) **8...0-0 9 ♕e2 c5?** (missing White's idea) **10 ♕e4!.**

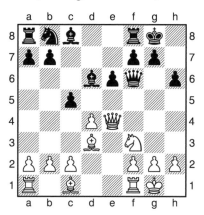

This seems like a crude mate threat. But Black turns out to have no good answer. Both 10...g6 and 10...♕g6 lose a pawn in simple fashion, while 10...♖d8 11 dxc5 ♗xc5 12 ♕h7+ ♔f8 13 ♗d2 intending ♗c3 gives White a devastating attack. With **10...♕f5 11 ♕h4 ♕f6** Black offers up a pawn to reduce the pressure. But White is having none of it: after **12 ♗g5!** the black queen is trapped by the same pattern of bishops and pawns as we saw in the previous example. The g5-bishop is untouchable because of the mate after **12...hxg5 13 ♕h7#**.

A Mousetrap for Rooks

Just a normal way to protect a knight's pawn

A rook proudly snatches a loose pawn on b7. But then the trap closes: a black knight (or bishop) appears on b6, blocking the rook's route back. Sometimes the rook has a way out, but other times, no matter how much it thrashes about, it will be captured in the end.

1 d4 d5 2 c4 e6 3 ♘c3 ♗e7 4 ♘f3 ♘f6 5 ♗g5 0-0 6 e3 h6 7 ♗h4 ♘e4 (this is the Lasker Defence in the Queen's Gambit Declined) **8 ♗xe7 ♕xe7 9 cxd5 ♘xc3 10 bxc3 exd5 11 ♗d3 ♗g4 12 ♖b1** and now **12...♘d7** demonstrates an important idea that is a standard way to 'defend' a b-pawn.

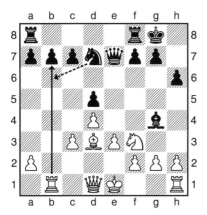

In most games, White wisely leaves the pawn alone. But in an under-12 event, she was tempted by the 'cheese': **13 ♖xb7??** **♘b6 14 ♕b3 ♗c8** and the rook is lost. An attempt to get a second pawn for the exchange failed: **15 ♖xb6 axb6! 16 ♕xd5 ♗e6 17 ♕e4** (threatening mate!) **17...f5 18 ♕e5 ♖a5** and Black soon won.

Sometimes the mousetrap snaps shut in higher-level games too. Here a grandmaster grabbed the b-pawn: **1 d4 ♘f6 2 c4 g6 3 ♘c3 d5 4 ♗g5 ♘e4 5 ♗h4 ♘xc3 6 bxc3 dxc4 7 e3 ♗e6 8 ♖b1 ♗g7 9 ♘h3 ♘d7 10 ♘f4 ♗f5**.

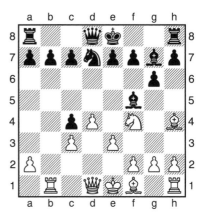

11 ♖xb7? (White should play the simple 11 ♖b2 or the crazily complex 11 ♗xc4 ♗xb1 12 ♗xf7+ ♔xf7 13 ♕b3+) **11...♘b6**.

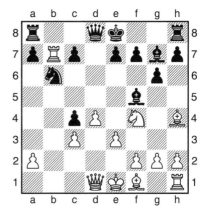

White had surely seen this but overestimated his attacking chances. After **12 ♕f3 0-0 13 ♗e2 ♕c8 14 ♖xb6 axb6 15 ♘d5 ♔h8 16 e4 ♗e6 17 ♘xe7 ♕d7** Black went on win.

TRAP 47

Stealing the Cheese

How to get the trap to jam

Having studied the mousetrap, we shall now see how the cheese can sometimes be stolen!

1 c4 ♘f6 2 ♘c3 d5 3 cxd5 ♘xd5 4 g3 g6 5 ♗g2 ♘xc3 6 bxc3 ♗g7 7 ♖b1 is a popular line of the English Opening. Now 7...♘d7 is a standard move, based on the 'Mousetrap' theme: 8 ♗xb7?? ♗xb7 9 ♖xb7 ♘b6 traps the rook. But in playing **7...0-0**, Black's main idea is that the obvious 8 ♗xb7?? ♗xb7 9 ♖xb7 doesn't win a pawn but in fact loses a rook after 9...♕d5!, forking the two rooks on the long diagonal – compare this with the *Uncompleted Fianchetto* (Trap 72). By simply castling, Black hopes to develop his remaining pieces to their ideal squares. But he is in for a surprise! With **8 ♗xb7!**, White turns the trap on its head.

he has lost. But a pawn up is better than a pawn down, and White has the better game whether he chooses 11 ♘f3 or 11 f3. So why didn't I give 7...0-0 a question mark? Well, it has been played more than once in recent years by a very strong grandmaster from China. He didn't score very well with it, but showed that with accurate play Black has good drawing chances. That such an 'obvious error' might actually be OK is a demonstration of the richness of chess. But don't try this at home!

Here is another example, from a different opening: **1 e4 c5 2 f4 ♘c6 3 ♘f3 g6 4 ♗b5 ♗g7 5 ♗xc6 bxc6 6 d3 d6 7 0-0 ♖b8**. Now with **8 ♕e1?!** White chooses to defend his pawn tactically.

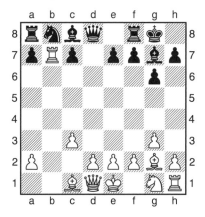

By willingly giving up his rook, White makes sure that his bishop will reign supreme on the long diagonal. Black has little choice about his next two moves, as otherwise he has lost an important pawn for nothing. **8...♗xb7 9 ♗xb7 ♘d7 10 ♗xa8 ♕xa8**. Black has some play for the material

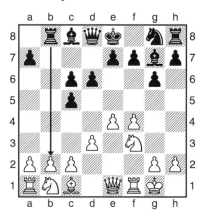

But we already know why this doesn't work: **8...♖xb2!** (not 8...♗xb2?? 9 ♗xb2 ♖xb2 10 ♕c3!) **9 ♗xb2 ♗xb2 10 ♘bd2 ♗xa1 11 ♕xa1 f6** leaves Black a pawn ahead, though with some defending to do.

TRAP 48   Carelessly Allowing the ♗xf7+ Sacrifice

The tactics radar is on, but no one is home

In standard-looking positions, players often forget to check for basic tactics. But a tiny change in the position of a single piece can make a safe position into a disaster.

1 e4 e5 2 ♘f3 ♘c6 3 ♗b5 a6 4 ♗a4 ♘f6 5 0-0 ♗e7 6 ♖e1 b5 7 ♗b3 d6 8 c3 0-0 9 h3 ♘b8 10 d4 ♘bd7 11 ♘bd2. This is a normal position in the Ruy Lopez. Thousands of games have continued 11...♗b7 12 ♗c2 ♖e8, leading to a complex middlegame battle. But players sometimes get careless, and churn out the moves without stopping to think. Still, it is shocking that **11...♖e8??** has been played more than a dozen times at master level, and often gone unpunished.

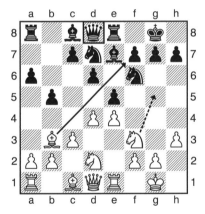

One game between masters in early 2018 featured the moves 12 ♘g5?? ♖f8 13 ♘gf3 ♖e8?? 14 ♘g5?? ♖f8 15 ♘gf3 ♖e8??, with the players agreeing a draw in a position where White again has a simple win. Look at the position as if you had never seen it before, and the problem is obvious. In fact, we saw an almost identical idea in Trap 16: **12 ♗xf7+!** wins on the spot because **12...♔xf7** (otherwise Black loses a pawn and a rook

for a bishop) **13 ♘g5+ ♔g8 14 ♘e6** traps the black queen because the bishop is still on c8. Never forget about tactics!

Now let's see a deeper idea. **1 e4 e5 2 ♘f3 d6 3 d4 ♘d7 4 ♗c4 c6 5 ♘g5 ♘h6** and with **6 a4** White sets a cunning trap.

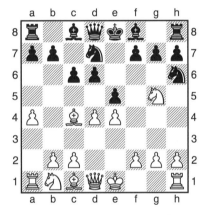

It looks like the black queen has plenty of squares, but there is some real danger. Now 6...exd4 is best, giving Black's knight the e5-square. But **6...♗e7??** takes one escape-route away from the queen and after **7 ♗xf7+! ♘xf7 8 ♘e6** White's a-pawn does the rest of the work: **8...♕b6** (or 8...♕a5+ 9 ♗d2 ♕b6 10 a5 ♕xb2 11 ♗c3 ♕b5 12 ♘c7+) **9 a5 ♕b4+ 10 c3 ♕c4 11 ♘c7+ ♔d8 12 b3** and the black queen is lost. This trap has claimed about 20 victims, including some rather strong players. In order to see through it, Black would need a good sense of danger and to think about why White had pushed his a-pawn.

61

TRAP 49 — Fischer's ♗xf7+ and ♘e6 Idea

Decoy, decoy, mate!

This spectacular way to drag out the enemy king should be familiar to those who have seen a Fischer-Reshevsky game that is quoted in a lot of beginners' books.

1 e4 e5 2 ♘f3 d6 3 ♗c4 (3 d4 can reach the same position following 3...♘d7 4 ♗c4 exd4 5 ♘xd4 ♗e7?? or 3...exd4 4 ♘xd4 ♗e7 5 ♗c4 ♘d7??) **3...♗e7 4 d4 exd4** (avoiding the well-known blunder 4...♘d7??, when 5 dxe5 wins at least a pawn by a direct attack on f7: 5...dxe5 6 ♕d5 or 5...♘xe5 6 ♘xe5 dxe5 7 ♕h5) **5 ♘xd4** and now Black should play 5...♘f6 and castle. **5...♘d7??** is still not safe because White breaks through on f7 in a different way:

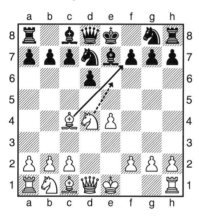

6 ♗xf7+! ♔xf7 7 ♘e6!. If Black takes the knight, he is mated: **7...♔xe6 8 ♕d5+ ♔f6 9 ♕f5#**. But leaving the knight on e6 is not much better: **7...♕e8 8 ♘xc7 ♕f8** (8...♕d8 loses more simply: 9 ♕d5+ ♔f8 10 ♘e6+) **9 ♕h5+ g6 10 ♕d5+ ♔f6 11 ♗g5+ ♔g7 12 ♘e6+** and the black queen finally falls. This all happened in a game played in Italy in the 1920s.

Now let's see a simplified version of the Fischer idea itself. After **1 e4 c5 2 ♘f3 g6 3 d4 ♗g7 4 ♗c4 cxd4 5 ♘xd4 ♘f6 6 ♘c3 0-0 7 0-0** Black has various good options, including the fork trick 7...♘xe4 8 ♘xe4 d5. Instead **7...b6??** takes two flight-squares away from the black queen. But why should that matter? It still has two squares and it seems there's no way for White to attack it.

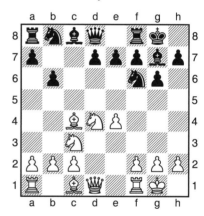

8 e5 ♘e8. That's one more flight-square occupied... (Instead 8...♘h5 9 g4 costs Black a piece.) **9 ♗xf7+!** (the point is to give the knight access to e6) **9...♔xf7** (9...♖xf7 10 ♘e6 traps the queen) **10 ♘e6!!** (making spectacular use of the pin on the d-file) **10...♔xe6** (10...dxe6 11 ♕xd8 gives Black just two pieces for the queen) **11 ♕d5+ ♔f5** offers White several ways to mate; e.g., **12 e6+ ♗e5 13 f4 ♕c7 14 fxe5+ ♔g4 15 h3+ ♔g3 16 ♘e4+ ♔h4 17 ♗g5+ ♔h5 18 g4#**.

TRAP 50 — Drag the King Out with ♘xf7

A can opener shaped like a horse

Sometimes players leave f7 so weak that a knight sacrifice on that square wins by force. The signs to look out for are a queen that can invade on e6 and other pieces ready to support the raid.

1 d4 e6 2 e4 b6 3 ♘c3 ♗b7 4 ♗d3 ♘f6 5 ♘f3 d5 6 exd5 exd5 7 0-0 ♗e7 8 ♖e1 0-0 9 ♕e2 ♖e8 10 ♗g5 ♘bd7 11 ♘e5 and now the careless move **11...h6?** was made by a German grandmaster, allowing one of his lower-ranked countrymen to score a cherished victory over him:

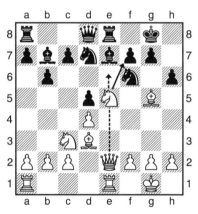

12 ♘xf7! ♕c8. After 12...♔xf7 the finish is 13 ♕e6+ ♔f8 14 ♗g6 and ♕f7# is unstoppable. **13 ♕e6!**. White has a number of good moves, but chooses the nicest finish. **13...♗f8 14 ♘xh6++ ♔h8 15 ♕g8+!**. A slight twist on the standard 'Philidor's Legacy' theme. After **15...♘xg8 16 ♘f7#** the black knight blocks g8 and the white bishop covers h7.

In the next example, rather than Black making a completely 'unforced error', White barraged him with threats, and this caused him to slip up. After **1 e4 e6 2 d4 d5 3 ♘d2 dxe4 4 ♘xe4 ♘d7 5 ♗d3 ♘gf6 6 ♕e2 ♗e7 7 ♘f3 0-0 8 0-0 b6 9 ♘eg5** White threatens 10 ♘xh7 ♘xh7 11 ♕e4 (exploiting the *Uncompleted Fianchetto*, a theme we explore in Trap 72), but Black's next move defends against this. **9...♗b7 10 ♖e1**.

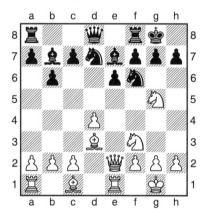

With the rook supporting the queen on the e-file, the threat is now 11 ♘xe6 fxe6 12 ♕xe6+ ♔h8 (or 12...♖f7 13 ♘g5) 13 ♕xe7. So Black puts his rook on the e-file too, but this allows a winning sacrifice on a different square. **10...♖e8?** (the black bishop should flee the e-file with 10...♗b4! 11 c3 ♗d6) **11 ♘xf7! ♔xf7** (11...♗xf3 changes little; then 12 gxf3 ♔xf7 13 ♕xe6+ ♔f8 14 ♗c4 was the finish of a game won by Capablanca – World Champion 1921-7 – in a simultaneous display) **12 ♘g5+ ♔g8 13 ♕xe6+** and now in a Polish game, Black sportingly allowed his opponent to execute the standard but beautiful mating finish: **13...♔h8 14 ♘f7+ ♔g8 15 ♘h6++ ♔h8 16 ♕g8+ ♘xg8 17 ♘f7#**.

63

Oh, the humanity! That poor defenceless pawn!

Castling queenside may make the king safe, but it does nothing to cover the f2 (or f7) square – in fact, it removes the king's defence of this vulnerable pawn.

Sometimes we can simply walk in and take the pawn: **1 d4 ♘f6 2 ♘f3 g6 3 ♘c3 d5 4 ♗f4 ♗g7 5 ♕d2** (this crude system of development has recently been named the 'Tarzan Attack' for some reason) **5...0-0 6 ♗h6 ♗xh6 7 ♕xh6 c5 8 0-0-0?** (8 dxc5 d4 9 0-0-0 ♘g4 is annoying, so 8 e3 seems best) **8...♘g4!**. Black pinpoints f2 as a major weakness. It is hard to defend, and if the knight lands there it will fork the white rooks. **9 ♕h4 e5!**.

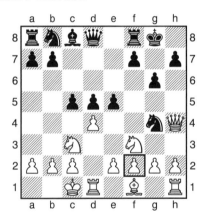

Black diverts the white queen from defending f2. After **10 ♕xd8 ♖xd8 11 dxe5 ♗e6** White is simply losing the f2-pawn, as **12 ♘e4?? ♘d7** just makes things worse. This trap has claimed a number of high-rated victims, including a Soviet grandmaster.

Normally a tactic is needed to exploit the weakness of f2/f7: **1 e4 e6 2 d4 d5 3 ♘c3 ♗b4 4 e5 c5 5 a3 ♗xc3+ 6 bxc3 ♘e7 7 ♘f3 ♕a5 8 ♗d2 ♗d7 9 ♗d3 c4 10 ♗f1**. With such a blocked position, quality development can be more important than fast development. White sees a good post for this bishop on h3. **10...♗a4 11 g3 ♘bc6 12 ♗h3 0-0-0??**.

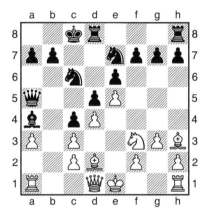

This leaves f7 fatally weak. Why? Because **13 ♘g5!** forces **13...♖df8** and after **14 ♘xf7! ♖xf7 15 ♗xe6+** the bishop delivers a decisive fork.

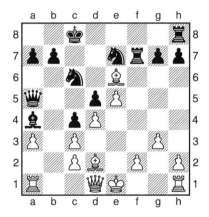

This was a game played at the famous Manhattan Chess Club in New York.

f7: Undefended Yet Again

Dodging the bullet once may not be enough

We have already seen positions where f7 was so exposed that a simple attack on this square brought the defences crashing down. The idea crops up often, so we should look at more examples.

With the clever move-order **1 e4 d6 2 d4 ♘f6 3 ♘c3 e5 4 ♘f3 ♘bd7**, Black avoids some of the normal problems that Black has with f7 in Philidor's Defence (see Traps 9, 48 and 49). But he still needs to be careful. **5 ♗c4 c6?**. Black gives his queen room, but defending the f7-pawn is a more urgent matter. 5...♗e7 is the normal move, played in thousands of games. Then 6 ♘g5 achieves little after 6...0-0 since 7 ♗xf7+ ♖xf7 8 ♘e6 does not trap the queen.

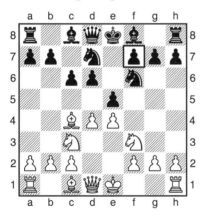

6 dxe5!. This is the cleanest way forward, but 6 ♘g5 is also strong. **6...dxe5**. After 6...♘xe5 7 ♘xe5 dxe5 the standard *deflection* sacrifice 8 ♗xf7+! wins a pawn for nothing. **7 ♘g5**. White attacks f7 and Black has no way to defend it – no need for any fancy tactics here. Black loses a pawn and more, as the knight lands on f7 with a fork. **7...♗b4 8 ♘xf7 ♕a5** tries to make a fight of it, but after **9 ♘xh8 ♗xc3+** the

sneaky sidestep **10 ♔f1!** leaves Black empty-handed.

In the next example, Black has castled and f7 looks well-protected, but the key defender can be driven away. **1 d4 g6 2 e4 d6 3 ♘c3 ♘f6 4 ♘f3 ♗g7 5 ♗e3 0-0 6 ♕d2 ♗g4** (oddly, 6...e5 is OK here) **7 ♘g5!?**. White wants to keep this useful knight. He plans to play h3 and after the bishop drops back, the knight can return to its excellent post on f3 if needed. With **7...e5??** Black strikes at the centre while it lacks the knight's protection.

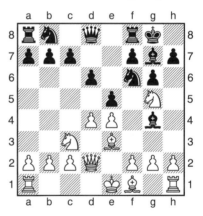

However, there is a problem that becomes clear after a few forced exchanges. **8 dxe5 dxe5 9 ♕xd8 ♖xd8 10 ♗c4!** **♖f8** (10...♖d7 blocks the bishop's route back, so 11 h3 ♗h5 12 g4 wins a piece) **11 ♗c5**. The rook has run out of squares, so Black must either let f7 collapse or lose the exchange (i.e. rook for bishop). This occurred in a game where future-grandmaster Aagaard was Black.

Castling Into It: Allowing ♗xh7+

Learn the warning signs and check if the ramparts will hold

Sometimes a player carelessly castles directly into an instantly winning Greek Gift sacrifice. Most players know about this sacrifice, but not everyone understands what features are necessary for it to work. These include a white queen and knight ready to swoop in, and normally a white pawn on e5. This is often the case in the French Defence, as we are about to see.

1 e4 e6 2 d4 d5 3 ♘d2 ♘f6 4 ♗d3 c5 5 c3 ♘c6 6 ♘gf3 cxd4 7 cxd4 ♗b4?!. Black is too eager to close the centre. 7...dxe4 8 ♘xe4 ♗e7 gives him a satisfactory game, with prospects of play against White's isolated pawn. **8 e5 ♘d7 9 0-0 ♕b6 10 ♘b3 0-0??**. Castling at this point is a terrible mistake, as it is clear that the sacrifice wins here. Black lacks defenders, while White's pieces are ready to pounce.

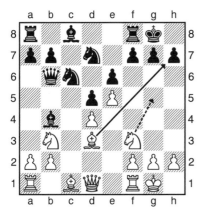

11 ♗xh7+! ♔xh7 (11...♔h8 12 ♘g5 is even worse) **12 ♘g5+** (if only Black's bishop were on a more useful square, such as e7!). Now **12...♔g8 13 ♕h5 ♖d8 14 ♕xf7+ ♔h8 15 ♕h5+ ♔g8 16 ♕h7+ ♔f8 17 ♕h8+ ♔e7 18 ♕xg7+ ♔e8 19 ♕f7#** is a standard mating sequence from the Greek Gift. **12...♔g6** gives White a few tempting options, such as 13 ♕d3+! f5 14 ♕h3, when Black must give

up a piece and more just to avoid instant mate.

Here's another example, also from the French Defence. Most of the pieces are on different squares, but the Greek Gift still works when Black fails to give his castled king enough defence: **1 e4 e6 2 d4 d5 3 ♘c3 ♘f6 4 ♗g5 ♗e7 5 e5 ♘e4 6 ♗xe7 ♕xe7 7 ♗d3** (7 ♘xe4! dxe4 8 ♕e2 gives Black problems with his exposed e4-pawn) **7...♘xc3 8 bxc3 c5 9 ♕g4 0-0 10 ♘f3**.

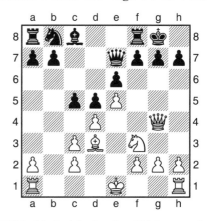

With this knight in play, White now has a threat, as his key attacking pieces are in place. **10...c4??**. Black decides to call White's bluff – but it was no bluff! 10...h6 is one way to defend, while 10...f5 is playable too. **11 ♗xh7+!** ♔xh7 **12 ♕h5+ ♔g8 13 ♘g5** and Black has a grim choice between being mated on the spot or losing his queen.

TRAP 54

Anastasia's Mate

Life and death at the edge of the board

Anastasia's Mate is a beautiful checkmate pattern at the edge of the board. It doesn't occur too often in the opening, but it is likely to crop up at some point in your games, particularly in the middlegame. If you are familiar with this mating idea, it is more likely to be you proudly delivering mate, rather than being shocked by it.

The position after **1 e4 e5 2 ♘f3 ♘c6 3 ♗b5 a6 4 ♗a4 ♘f6 5 0-0 ♘xe4 6 ♖e1 ♘c5** should be completely OK for Black, but there are some nasty traps for him to avoid, such as this: **7 ♘c3 ♘xa4 8 ♘xe5 ♘xe5??** (a 'popular' blunder, but 8...♗e7 is forced) **9 ♖xe5+ ♗e7 10 ♘d5 0-0 11 ♘xe7+ ♔h8**. It appears that the players have simply made an odd-looking exchange of pieces, but White conjures up a mating attack with **12 ♕h5!**.

The mating pieces don't have to be a rook and knight; a queen is more than good enough, and it can be the knight that actually gives mate. **1 e4 e5 2 ♘f3 ♘c6 3 ♗c4 ♘f6 4 ♘g5 d5 5 exd5 ♘d4 6 c3 b5 7 ♗f1 ♘xd5 8 cxd4 ♕xg5 9 ♗xb5+ ♔d8 10 ♕f3 e4 11 ♕xe4 ♗d6 12 0-0 ♗b7** once occurred in a simultaneous display with Fischer playing White.

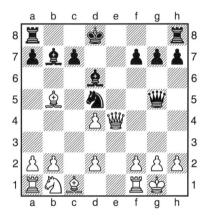

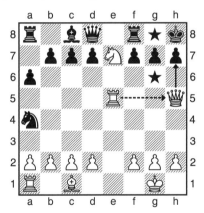

12...d6. This allows White's main idea, but 12...g6 13 ♕h4 and 12...h6 13 d4 followed by ♗xh6 are also winning for White. **13 ♕xh7+ ♔xh7 14 ♖h5#**. This is the classic mate pattern, with the knight covering both of the king's flight-squares so the rook can deliver mate along the edge of the board.

He chose **13 d3??**, but then noticed that this allowed Black to win by **13...♗xh2+!** (in the game, Black missed his chance with 13...♘f4??) **14 ♔xh2 ♘f4**. The main point is **15 ♕xb7** (15 ♗xf4 ♕h5+ 16 ♔g1 ♗xe4 doesn't give White enough for the queen) **15...♕h4+ 16 ♔g1 ♘e2#**, a pattern closely related to Anastasia's Mate.

67

TRAP 55 &xh7+ Setting Up a Queen Fork

A queen can attack h7 and any other square on the board

A &xh7+ sacrifice isn't always a Greek Gift or a discovered attack. There can be many other reasons why it is a good move. Sometimes it sets up a fork by the queen – all it needs is one loose piece that it can hit while checking the king on h7. There are a huge number of ways this idea can work, so view these two examples as inspiration rather than set-ups to be memorized.

1 d4 &f6 2 &f3 e6 3 e3 b6 4 &d3 &b7 5 0-0 &e7 6 c4 &e4 7 &c3 f5 8 d5 &xc3 9 bxc3 &f6 10 &d4 exd5 11 cxd5 &xd5 12 &xf5. The opening play so far has been fairly ordinary, though having opened the centre, Black should be on high tactical alert. However...

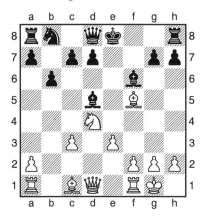

12...0-0?? 13 &xh7+! &xh7 14 ₩h5+ (forking king and bishop) **14...&g8 15 ₩xd5+.** White has not just won a pawn, but a whole rook too, with this second queen fork.

The second example is more complex. **1 e4 e6 2 d4 d5 3 exd5 exd5 4 c4 &f6 5 &c3 &b4 6 &f3 0-0 7 &d3 ₤e8+.** This looks like an inconvenient check, but White has a good answer. **8 &e3 &g4?!** (the point, but Black should instead develop his queenside pieces) **9 0-0!.** Now 9...&xe3 10 fxe3 allows White excellent play along the f-file and 9...&xc3 10 bxc3 ₤xe3? 11 fxe3 &xe3 12 ₩e2! &xf1

13 &g5 gives White too many threats. But Black thought he could do better with a 'clever' exchange sacrifice: **9...₤xe3? 10 fxe3 &xe3.**

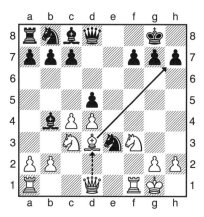

11 &xh7+! &xh7 12 ₩d3+ (the queen fork) **12...&f5 13 &xd5 &e7 14 g4** and White makes decisive material gains.

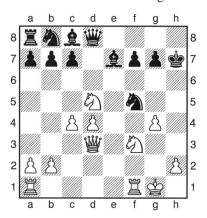

TRAP 56

Queen Invasion after ...♘xg2

A neat way to blast open the front door

A knight sacrifice on g2 (or g7) can be a great way to bring the queen into an attack. Even when the idea is relatively simple, it is easy to miss, as our first example shows.

1 d4 ♘f6 2 ♘f3 g6 3 c4 ♗g7 4 ♘c3 0-0 5 e4 d6 6 ♗e2 e5 7 0-0 ♘a6 8 ♗e3 ♘g4 9 ♗g5 ♕e8 10 h3 h6 11 ♗c1 ♘f6 12 dxe5 dxe5 13 ♗e3 ♘h5 14 c5 ♘f4 is a known sequence in the King's Indian Defence. **15 ♗b5 ♕e6**. With hindsight, Black's ideas of ...♘xg2 seem clear. But when this position arose in one of his games, Alexei Shirov, top grandmaster and amazing tactician, not only missed it, but made it far stronger: **16 ♕a4?? ♘xg2!**.

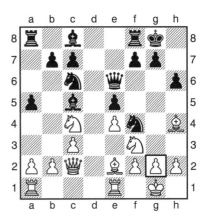

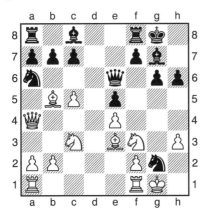

17 ♔xg2 ♕xh3+ 18 ♔g1 ♕g4+ 19 ♔h2 ♕xf3. Igor Glek, the grandmaster playing Black, had now won two pawns and still had attacking chances. It was just a matter of time before he won the game.

The next example features cautious play by White, but he still falls victim to this theme. **1 e4 e5 2 ♘f3 ♘c6 3 c3 ♘f6 4 d3 d5 5 ♕c2 a5 6 ♗e2 ♗c5 7 0-0 0-0 8 ♗g5 dxe4 9 dxe4 h6 10 ♗h4 ♕d6 11 ♘bd2 ♘h5 12 ♘c4 ♕e6 13 ♖fe1 ♘f4**.

The queen and knight are in position. White defended g2 with **14 ♗f1?**, but this doesn't help: **14...♘xg2!** *overloads* the f1-bishop. **15 ♗xg2** allows **15...♕xc4**, while **15 ♔xg2 ♕h3+ 16 ♔g1 ♕xf3** left White a pawn down with a weak kingside in another high-level game.

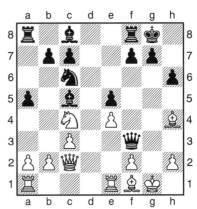

So watch out for knight sacrifices on g2 or g7, or you might be caught unawares too.

Paralysing Pins

The right pin in the wrong place can make all the difference

In this book we see many powerful pins. Sometimes they win a piece, or they paralyse a piece for many moves because there is no way to break the pin. Here we look at pins that are fleeting – like a snowflake – but last just long enough to allow some evil tactic.

1 e4 c5 2 d4 cxd4 3 c3 dxc3 4 ♘xc3 ♘c6 5 ♘f3 d6 6 ♗c4 a6 7 ♗g5. The white bishop appears to be floating in mid-air without any good reason. Is it preparing to exchange the black knight if it moves to f6, doubling Black's pawns? Yes, but there is also a deadlier plan. Can you see White's threat? **7...h6??**. Black should just play 7...♘f6 8 ♗xf6 gxf6, when his extra pawn is doubled, but still of value.

There the bishop pinned a key pawn. A more typical case is the bishop pinning a knight on e7, gumming up the defences and bringing in ideas of a smothered mate. **1 e4 c5 2 d4 cxd4 3 c3 dxc3 4 ♘xc3 ♘c6 5 ♗c4 e6 6 ♘f3 ♘ge7 7 ♗g5 a6 8 e5?!**. Once again: do you see White's threat? **8...h6??** is a classic case of assuming an attacked piece must move away.

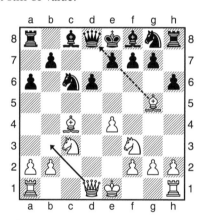

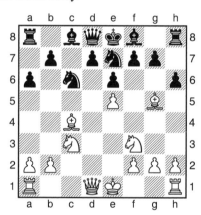

8 ♕b3!. That's right, the bishop is pinning the pawn on e7, so this attack on f7 is devastating. It doesn't matter that the bishop will die on g5 – it lives just long enough. After 8...hxg5 9 ♗xf7+ ♔d7 10 ♗xg8 White wins back the piece while leaving Black's defences in ruins. **8...♗e6** fails because after **9 ♗xe6 fxe6 10 ♗e3** Black can't defend both pawns with **10...♕d7** because of **11 ♘a4** and ♘b6.

But White just carries out his threat: **9 ♘e4!**. Now 9...hxg5? allows 10 ♘d6#, but the knight is invading on d6 in any case. 9...♕c7? 10 ♘d6+ ♔d8 11 ♘xf7+ ♔e8 gives White many good options, including 12 ♘xh8. So **9...d5** is forced, but then **10 exd6 hxg5 11 d7+!** is a powerful *square-vacation*. **11...♗xd7?** 12 ♘d6# is smothered mate, and 11...♕xd7 12 ♘d6+ ♕xd6 (12...♔d8 13 ♘xf7+) 13 ♕xd6 gives Black only two pieces for the queen.

Levenfish Trap and Relatives

A queen hooks a knight using a pin

A well-known trap in the Sicilian is based on briefly pinning a bishop so that the white queen can take a loose knight on g4. This idea can also be transplanted to other openings.

1 e4 c5 2 ♘f3 d6 3 d4 cxd4 4 ♘xd4 ♘f6 5 ♘c3 g6 is the Dragon Variation of the Sicilian. A basic trap is now 6 ♗e3 ♘g4?? 7 ♗b5+! ♗d7 8 ♕xg4, when White wins a piece. Bear this in mind while we look at **6 f4**, which is known as the Levenfish Attack. Knowledgeable Dragon players don't fear it at all, but if Black plays the most obvious moves, he can land quickly in trouble. **6...♗g7** (6...♘c6 is the simplest way to avoid any danger) **7 e5 dxe5?!** (7...♘g4? 8 ♗b5+ forces the king to move – even though Black doesn't lose his queen here, his development is a mess; 7...♘h5 is the best chance at this point) **8 fxe5 ♘g4?** (8...♘fd7 9 e6! gives Black problems but the game is not over).

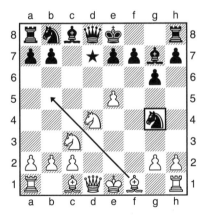

9 ♗b5+! ♔f8?? (9...♗d7? 10 ♕xg4 is the familiar idea, while 9...♘c6 10 ♘xc6 costs Black at least a pawn) **10 ♘e6+** and the black queen is lost. This is the 'Levenfish Trap', and has claimed countless hundreds of victims. Even this position, where Black falls for it hook, line and sinker, has occurred well over a hundred times in recorded games.

1 e4 d6 2 d4 ♘f6 3 ♘c3 g6 (this is the Pirc Defence) **4 ♗g5 ♗g7 5 f4 c5 6 e5** is a very aggressive way for White to play. If Black doesn't know what he is doing (like I didn't in a rapidplay game in the Soviet Union one time!), he can quickly end up in deep trouble. **6...♘g4?** (6...dxe5 7 dxe5! gave me serious problems with the white knight coming into d5 in that game I mentioned; 6...♘h5 is best, with the idea of playing ...h6 and taking the pawn on f4) **7 ♗b5+!**.

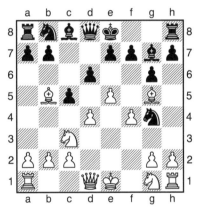

There is no good reply to this check. 7...♗d7? of course loses the knight to 8 ♕xg4. 7...♔f8 misplaces the king and allows 8 dxc5 thanks to the pin on the d-file. **7...♘c6** was chosen in a game in an old Soviet championship, where White missed the win of a piece by **8 d5! a6 9 dxc6! axb5 10 cxb7 ♗xb7 11 ♕xg4**.

TRAP 59 — Deadly Pins on the d-File

An open file is a two-way street

The d-file is a superhighway for pins. The queen starts the game on this file and a rook can quickly move there as part of queenside castling. That's a lot of firepower! A piece on the d-file can suddenly find itself pinned against its own queen. Let's see some typical examples.

1 e4 c5 2 ♘f3 ♘c6 3 d4 cxd4 4 ♘xd4 ♘f6 5 ♘c3 d6 6 ♗g5 e6 7 ♕d2 a6 8 0-0-0 is a standard position in the Sicilian Defence. Do you see White's threat? **8...♘xd4**. Black's most common moves are 8...♗d7 and 8...h6, which both avoid a disaster on the d-file. **9 ♕xd4**. If Black decides to start a queenside advance right away, he hits a problem: **9...b5?? 10 e5!**.

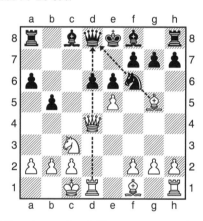

The pin on the d-file means the d6-pawn can't take on e5, so the knight is lost to a basic 'pin and win'. After **10...b4** (10...h6 now comes too late: 11 exf6 hxg5 12 fxg7 wins a piece) **11 ♘e4** Black is lost, as **11...d5** threatens nothing so White plays **12 exf6**.

Our second example is more subtle. White wins a pawn with a sneaky trick, but fails to spot that he has opened up the d-file for a deadly pin on his own knight. **1 ♘f3 e6 2 g3 b6 3 ♗g2 ♗b7 4 c4 f5 5 d4 ♘f6 6 0-0 ♗e7 7 d5 ♘a6 8 ♘d4 ♕c8 9 dxe6?! ♗xg2**

10 exd7+??. White tries to use the *Rampant Pawn* idea, but it is no good here. He should settle for 10 ♔xg2 dxe6, though these exchanges have helped Black gain a good game. **10...♕xd7 11 ♔xg2**.

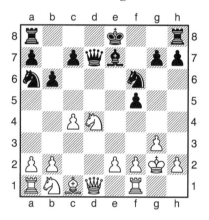

So, is White just a pawn up? **11...0-0-0!**. No! The pin will cost White his knight. In one game between masters, 12 ♕c2 ♕xd4 13 ♕xf5+ ♔b8 gave White nothing like enough for the piece, while after **12 e3 c5** the pawn adds the finishing touch. (Note that Black does actually need to castle to win the knight, since 11...♖d8? 12 ♘c3 ♕xd4 lets White pick off a black knight by 13 ♕a4+.)

There are two instructive points here:

1) A player trying to trick his opponent can easily miss a deadly trick in reply.

2) When White was deciding on his disastrous line of play, the d-file was closed, so the idea of a pin along it would have been hard to imagine.

72

Long Diagonal Pin

Always take central pawns. Except when you shouldn't

We see a great many pins in this book, but those on the long diagonals (a1-h8 and h1-a8) are particularly powerful. Firstly, there is a rook at the end of the diagonal – a juicy target. Also, these diagonals pass through the heart of the board – the central squares – so tactics in all parts of the board tend to accompany the pin.

1 e4 e6 2 d3 d5 3 ♘d2 ♘f6 4 ♘gf3 ♗e7 5 g3 b6 6 ♗g2 ♗b7 7 0-0. It looks like White has forgotten about his pawn on e4, but he is setting a subtle trap. It is also a good move, as White prepares to support his e-pawn with ♖e1. **7...dxe4 8 dxe4 ♘xe4??**. Now 9 ♘g5? ♗xg5 10 ♘xe4 ♗xc1 gives White nothing clear, but with **9 ♘e5!** the trap is sprung.

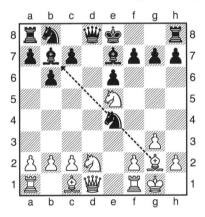

The pin on the long diagonal is deadly, together with threats against f7. 9...♗f6 10 ♘xe4 ♗xe5 11 ♘f6+ ♗xf6 12 ♕xd8+ ♔xd8 13 ♗xb7 will leave White at least rook for knight up. 9...♕d4 is met by 10 ♘xe4 ♕xe5 11 ♘f6+ and 12 ♗xb7. After 9...f5 10 ♗xe4 ♗xe4 11 ♕h5+ g6 12 ♘xg6 White will mate or make decisive material gains. With **9...♘d6** Black tries to defend everything, but **10 ♗xb7 ♘xb7 11 ♕f3** is a decisive double attack on b7 and f7.

After **1 d4 ♘f6 2 c4 e6 3 ♘f3 b6 4 g3 ♗a6 5 ♘bd2 ♗b7 6 ♗g2 ♗e7 7 0-0 c5** White can make the powerful central advance **8 e4!**. It is similar to the previous example, but not identical, so we must check the tactics still work. **8...♘xe4?? 9 ♘e5! d5**. This defends the knight, but exposes the king on the a4-e8 diagonal. (9...f5 10 ♗xe4 ♗xe4 11 ♕h5+ and 9...♘d6 10 ♗xb7 ♘xb7 11 ♕f3 are once again winning for White.) **10 cxd5!** gives Black big problems.

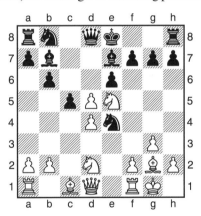

Now **10...exd5 11 ♕a4+ ♔f8** (or 11...♘d7 12 ♘xe4 dxe4 13 ♗h3) **12 ♘xe4 dxe4 13 dxc5** gives White a very powerful attack. Instead Black might think that **10...♘xd2** will save him, but then comes a surprise: **11 ♘xf7!** (we saw this idea in Trap 39) **11...♔xf7 12 dxe6+ ♔g8 13 ♗xb7** and White wins too much material.

Pinned Knight on the Rook's File

A ready-made pin – just remove the pawns

While the opening is all about fighting for the centre, it often happens that a rook's file (a-file or h-file) is opened up. And although you may have read that 'knights on the rim are dim', players find reasons to put them there, such as driving back a well-placed bishop. This sometimes leads to a knight being pinned on a rook's file with fatal consequences. Let's see how.

1 e4 e5 2 ♘f3 ♘c6 3 ♗b5 a6 4 ♗a4 ♘f6 5 0-0 b5 6 ♗b3 ♗e7 7 ♖e1 d6 8 c3 0-0 (8...♘a5 9 ♗c2 c5 10 a4 0-0?? is another move-order leading to the same position) **9 a4.** White attacks the b5-pawn – a standard ploy in this opening, the Ruy Lopez. **9...♘a5.** Black parries the threat of axb5, while planning to exchange off White's bishop. **10 ♗c2.** Instead 10 ♗a2 c5 is playable for Black, which might have led him to play ...c5 even when the bishop went to c2.

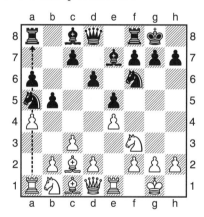

However, the position is different in a very important way: the bishop is not blocking the a-file, giving both sides extra ideas. **10...c5??** (10...b4 is better, planning 11 cxb4?! ♘c6 and ...♘xb4, since 12 b5?! axb5 turns the a-file pin against White) **11 axb5 axb5 12 b4!** This a-file pin has cost Black a piece in a number of games. In one of them, the player with Black was called Nutter.

Here is a similar idea in a totally different setting: **1 d4 d5 2 c4 dxc4 3 ♘f3 a6 4 a4 ♘c6 5 e3 ♘a5.** The knight moves to the edge to make it harder for White to recapture the pawn and to bring in ...♘b3 ideas. **6 ♘bd2 b5?.** Now White can open the a-file, with terrible consequences for the a5-knight. **7 axb5 axb5 8 b4! cxb3.** Even an *en passant* capture does not save Black. **9 ♗xb5+ ♗d7** (or 9...c6 10 ♗xc6+ ♘xc6 11 ♖xa8) **10 ♗xd7+ ♕xd7 11 ♘e5.**

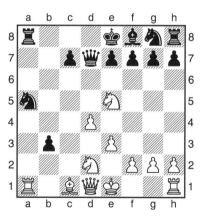

Now Black comes under assault from all angles. **11...♕d5** (11...♕c8 12 ♘xb3 ♘xb3 13 ♕f3 is a decisive double attack on a8 and f7) **12 ♘xb3 e6** (12...♘xb3 13 ♕xb3! ♕xb3 14 ♖xa8+ and mate next move) **13 0-0.** White's many threats include ♖xa5 followed by e4. For instance, **13...♘f6 14 ♖xa5 ♖xa5 15 e4 ♘xe4 16 ♘xa5 ♕xa5 17 ♕c2** and the queen invades.

TRAP 62 — More Pins

They come in all shapes and sizes

Pins are extremely common and appear in many forms. Here are two more. In the first it proves far harder for White to break the pin than he expected, thanks to some surprising tactics. The second is a pin against a key square where White wants to put a bishop to trap the black queen. It could also be viewed as a *line-opening* tactic. As always, what matters most is that it works!

After **1 c4 e5 2 ♘c3 ♘f6 3 ♘f3 d6 4 d4 e4 5 ♘d2 ♗f5 6 ♕c2 ♗g6, 7 ♘dxe4?** walks into a pin that causes White more problems than he bargained for. **7...♘xe4 8 ♘xe4 d5!**.

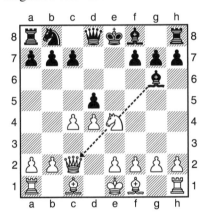

9 ♕a4+ b5!. Here we see the *...b5 Shocker* theme (see Trap 91), denying White time to save his knight, while drawing the queen further into unsafe territory. **10 ♕xb5+ c6 11 ♕b7 dxe4! 12 ♕xa8?**. And now the queen will be *Trapped in the Corner* after a forcing sequence of checks. This one game is almost an opening-trap encyclopaedia in itself! **12...♗b4+ 13 ♗d2 ♗xd2+ 14 ♔xd2 ♕xd4+ 15 ♔e1 ♕xb2 16 ♖d1 0-0 17 e3 ♗h5 18 f3 exf3 19 ♖d2 f2+** (White resigned here in an old Soviet game) **20 ♖xf2 ♕c1#**.

Let's go back to move 9 and look at **9 cxd5**, when **9...♕xd5? 10 ♘c3!** works well for White. But Black throws in the check

9...♗b4+! 10 ♗d2 (or 10 ♔d1 ♕xd5 and now 11 ♘c3? ♗xc2+ is check) **10...♗xd2+ 11 ♔xd2 ♕xd5 12 f3** (12 ♘c3? ♕xd4+) **12...♕xd4+ 13 ♔e1 ♗xe4**, which leads to a bad ending for White due to his broken pawns.

Our second example is simpler and more standard. **1 d4 d5 2 c4 e6 3 ♘c3 ♘f6 4 ♘f3 ♗e7 5 ♗g5 ♘bd7 6 cxd5 exd5 7 e3 c6 8 ♗d3 0-0 9 ♕c2 ♖e8 10 0-0 ♘e4 11 ♗f4** is a typical position from the Queen's Gambit. White is threatening a nasty trick that anyone who plays this opening must know. After **11...f5?? 12 ♘xd5!** White wins a key pawn.

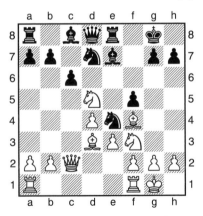

That's because **12...cxd5? 13 ♗c7** leaves the black queen trapped. The 'pin' here wasn't against a piece, but the c7-square, where White wanted to put his bishop. White's knight sacrifice *opened the c-file*.

Long Diagonal and Rook-Lift

A direct attack flowing straight from the opening

Some attacking plans spring directly from an opening set-up. Here we take a look at a brutal idea featuring a *rook-lift* that has caught many players unawares. All it takes is one slip by the defender and it is instant disaster!

1 b3 d5 2 ♗b2 ♘f6 3 ♘f3 c5 4 e3 ♘c6 5 ♗b5 e6 6 ♘e5 ♕c7 7 0-0 ♗d6 8 f4 0-0 9 ♗xc6 bxc6. Remember the set-up, rather than the sequence of moves. The brutal attacking manoeuvre we are about to see can be used by both White and Black, and with the pieces on slightly different squares. **10 ♖f3 ♘d7 11 ♖h3**.

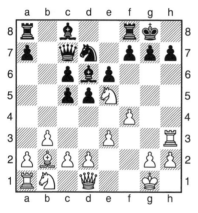

A rook advance followed by a sidewise move in front of its own pawns is called a 'rook-lift'. Like an air-drop, it gets heavy weapons into the thick of the action. White plans to bring in more firepower with ♕h5, so Black must react. **11...g6?**. This obvious way to prevent ♕h5 doesn't work at all! Black could avoid disaster by exchanging pieces on e5, but the best defence is 11...f6! 12 ♕h5 (12 ♘xd7 ♕xd7 leads to a complex middlegame in which Black shouldn't be worse) 12...fxe5 13 ♕xh7+ ♔f7 14 ♖g3.

Then White's attack compensates for the piece, but there is no knockout. A detailed analysis is beyond the scope of this book, but over the board the better player should win! **12 ♕h5!!**. Amazing! White plays the move Black just 'stopped' and sacrifices a whole queen. But if Black takes, he is mated: 12...gxh5 13 ♖g3+ ♔h8 14 ♘xf7# – a mighty double check and mate. **12...♘f6** prevents ♕xh7#, but is met by another stunning blow:

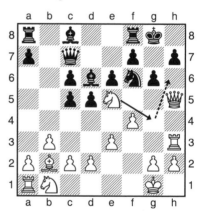

Now 13 ♕h6! is strong, but the most spectacular option is **13 ♘g4! gxh5** (13...♘xh5 allows 14 ♘h6#, while everything else is obviously hopeless) **14 ♘xf6+ ♔h8 15 ♖xh5!**. White threatens ♖xh7#, and 15...♔g7 16 ♘e8++ ♔g6 17 ♖g5+ ♔h6 18 ♗g7# is a pretty mate. 15...h6 is the only way to avoid mate, but after 16 ♘xd5+ White regains the queen, keeping several extra pawns.

TRAP 64   ♗xh7+: Invasion on f7

Leaving two key squares unprotected is asking for trouble

The ♗xh7+ sacrifice opens up the black king to all manner of attacking ideas. Sometimes the queen can invade on f7, particularly if there is a knight on e5 and the black rook has left f8.

1 e4 c6 2 d4 d5 3 ♘c3 dxe4 4 ♘xe4 ♘d7 5 ♘f3 ♘gf6 6 ♘g3 e6 7 ♗d3 ♗e7 8 0-0 0-0 9 ♘e5 ♖e8?!. Leaving f7 weak is a bad idea. 9...c5 10 c3 cxd4 11 cxd4 ♘d5 makes more sense. **10 ♖e1 c5 11 c3 cxd4 12 cxd4 ♘d5??**. Black is dreaming of playing ...♘7f6, firmly blockading the d4-pawn, but gets no time for this. (12...♘f8 makes use of the square the rook has left, and settles in for a long defence.)

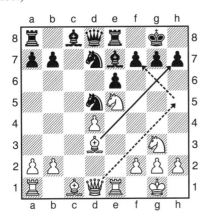

13 ♗xh7+! ♔xh7 14 ♕h5+ ♔g8 15 ♕xf7+. Now 15...♔h7 16 ♕g6+ ♔g8 17 ♕xe6+ ♔h7 18 ♕g6+ ♔g8 19 ♘f5 leads to mate, while 15...♔h8 offers White many ways to win, such as 16 ♘g6+ ♔h7 17 ♖xe6 (threatening ♘f8+ and ♖h6#) 17...♘7f6 18 ♘f5 ♖g8 19 ♘fxe7.

In the next example, White has to work a little harder to set up the same theme. **1 e4 e6 2 d4 d5 3 ♘c3 dxe4 4 ♘xe4 ♘d7 5 ♘f3 ♘gf6 6 ♘xf6+ ♘xf6 7 ♗d3 ♗e7 8 0-0 0-0 9 ♘e5**. White is very active and Black must be

careful. **9...c5 10 dxc5 ♕c7 11 ♖e1 ♕xc5 12 ♗g5 ♖d8??**.

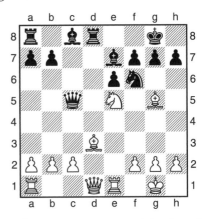

13 ♗xf6! (removing a defender of the h7-pawn) **13...♗xf6 14 ♗xh7+! ♔xh7 15 ♕h5+ ♔g8 16 ♕xf7+ ♔h7 17 ♖e3**. A rook-lift is a typical follow-up to the queen invasion on f7.

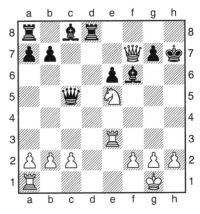

17...♖d4 is a desperate attempt to defend, but **18 g4!** wins by ruling out ...♖h4 ideas.

TRAP 65 ♘g5: Discovery on the Long Diagonal

So simple... and so easily missed

This double attack is made using three pieces (queen, bishop and knight) and on two diagonals that criss-cross almost the whole board.

1 ♘f3 ♘f6 2 g3 b6 3 d4 e6 4 ♗g2 ♗b7 5 0-0 ♗e7 6 c4 0-0 7 ♘c3 ♘e4 8 ♕c2 ♘xc3 9 ♕xc3 d6 and here **10 ♕d3** creates a threat that is obvious if you are aware of the idea. Black has several safe moves, such as 10...f5, 10...d5 and 10...♕c8. Otherwise Black might get a horrible surprise... **10...c5?? 11 ♘g5!.**

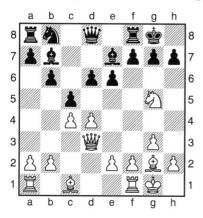

There are many forms of this ♘g5 theme. The common features are the threat on h7 and the loose black bishop on the long diagonal. The white queen is often on c2. The theme doesn't always work, and the tactical details need to be calculated. This is a simple case, where White wins cleanly. After **11...♗xg5 12 ♗xb7** the rook is trapped in the corner and Black suffers a decisive loss of material.

In our next example the target square is different. **1 d4 e6 2 ♘f3 ♘f6 3 c4 ♗b4+ 4 ♗d2 ♗xd2+ 5 ♕xd2 b6 6 g3 ♗b7 7 ♗g2 d6 8 ♘c3 ♘e4 9 ♕f4! ♘xc3??**. Maybe Black felt safe as White can't threaten mate on h7.

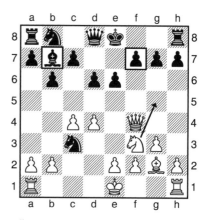

10 ♘g5!. But mate on f7 will do just as well! After **10...f6 11 ♗xb7 fxg5** White has a number of ways to win material, but there are still some interesting ideas; for example, **12 ♕e3 ♘d7 13 ♕xe6+ ♔f8 14 ♗xa8 ♕xa8.**

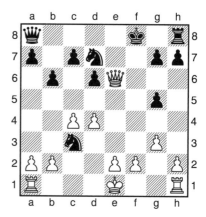

Now White must avoid 15 0-0?? ♕e4! 16 ♕xd7?? because of 16...♘xe2#, but after **15 f3** Black can't save both knights.

Legally Mated

Not such a useless theme to know!

Most beginners' books present Legall's Mate, an old but beautiful mate that, alas, you're not likely to see in games above beginner level nowadays. However, there are some ideas based on this mate that do occur in 'real' games.

1 e4 e5 2 ♘f3 ♘c6 3 ♘c3 d6 is a rare form of the Three Knights Game. Now 4 d4 exd4 5 ♘xd4 gives White a space advantage and it is hard for Black to develop actively with the pawn already on d6. The move **4 ♗c4** is also good, and invites a blunder. With **4...♗g4?!** Black gives meaning to his early ...d6, but there is a snag. After **5 h3!** Black has nothing better than exchanging on f3, but then White is ahead in development and has a pleasant strategic advantage: the *bishop-pair*. (Note that the immediate 5 ♘xe5?? is a blunder because 5...♗xe5 defends the bishop.)

There is a second key point that makes White's idea work: **6...♘xe5 7 ♕xh5 ♘xc4** (7...♘f6 8 ♕e2 leaves White a pawn up for nothing) and now the queen fork **8 ♕b5+** regains the piece, leaving White a good pawn ahead.

Some rather strong players have also fallen for the Legall theme in the King's Gambit: **1 e4 e5 2 f4 exf4 3 ♘f3 d6 4 ♗c4 h6 5 h4 ♘f6 6 ♘c3 ♗g4 7 d4 ♘h5?**. Black protects his extra pawn and eyes the weak g3-square, but there is a huge problem with this move. (7...♗e7 is safer, but unambitious.)

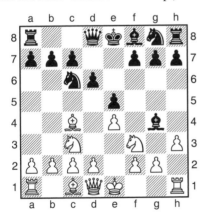

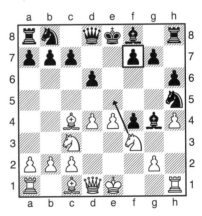

Shockingly, **5...♗h5??** is the most common move in practice here, and has even been played by masters. Equally shockingly, the winning move **6 ♘xe5!** is not the most common reply. Then **6...♗xd1?** allows the classic Legall Mate: **7 ♗xf7+ ♔e7 8 ♘d5#**.

8 ♘e5!! dxe5 (8...♗xd1?? 9 ♗xf7+ ♔e7 10 ♘d5# once occurred in a game played by mail!) **9 ♕xg4** and Black has nothing better than **9...♘f6 10 ♕f5 exd4** (10...♕xd4 11 ♕c8+) **11 ♘d5**, but White is in full command of the game.

TRAP 67 Spectacular Smothered Mates

No double check needed here – so double check for it!

We have already seen a number of smothered mate patterns (Traps 1, 5, 23, 37, 50 and 57). The one we now look at happens in the corner (like Philidor's Legacy), but the method is different.

1 e4 c5 2 ♘f3 ♘f6 3 e5 ♘d5 4 ♘c3 e6 5 ♘xd5 exd5 6 d4 ♘c6 7 dxc5 ♗xc5 8 ♕xd5 ♕b6 9 ♗c4 ♗xf2+ 10 ♔e2 0-0 11 ♖f1 ♗c5. In an unusual opening, both players offered pawn sacrifices for rapid development, but White's attack is the stronger. **12 ♘g5! ♘d4+ 13 ♔d1 ♘e6 14 ♘e4**. Black has covered the f7-square, so White tries to stop Black developing his queenside pieces. **14...d6 15 exd6 ♗xd6??**. Black thinks he has found a way out, but loses because of a beautiful mate. **16 ♘xd6 ♖d8**. It seems Black will take on d6 and White's queen must flee.

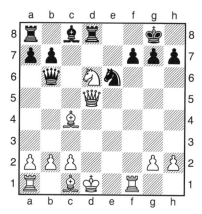

17 ♗f4!!. It's not instantly clear why this helps, as Black can simply take the bishop. **17...♘xf4 18 ♕xf7+ ♔h8 19 ♕g8+!**. The point is revealed. The queen both lures the rook to a square where it blocks the king, and also deflects it away from d8, unpinning the knight so it can deliver mate. **19...♖xg8**

20 ♘f7#. This clever point has won a number of games over the last fifty years, all the way up to grandmaster level.

1 e4 e5 2 ♘f3 ♘c6 3 ♗b5 a6 4 ♗a4 ♘f6 5 0-0 ♘xe4 6 d4 ♗e7 7 ♖e1 f5 (a risky plan for Black, as the open a2-g8 diagonal will leave his king exposed) **8 dxe5 0-0 9 ♗b3+ ♔h8 10 ♘c3 d6 11 exd6 ♗xd6 12 ♘xe4 fxe4 13 ♘g5 ♗f5**. Now 14 ♘f7+?! ♖xf7 15 ♗xf7 ♘e5 gives Black excellent play against the white king. **14 ♕d5!?** is more cunning.

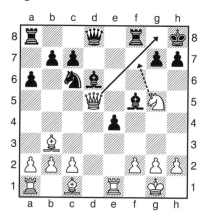

It looks like White is intending ♘f7+, but there is a far nastier threat too. Having two threats makes it more likely for the opponent to miss one of them. With **14...♘d4??** Black deals with the obvious idea, since 15 ♘f7+?? ♖xf7 16 ♕xf7 ♕h4 now gives Black a winning attack. And 15 ♕xd4?? ♗xh2+ is a simple queen win, as in Trap 8. But **15 ♕g8+! ♖xg8 16 ♘f7#** mates.

Decoy and Double Check

Drag the enemy king into the crossfire at any cost

The double check is such a fearsome weapon that it is often worth a major material sacrifice to *decoy* the enemy king into one.

There is a famous game between Réti and Tartakower that went **1 e4 c6 2 d4 d5 3 ♘c3 dxe4 4 ♘xe4 ♘f6 5 ♕d3 e5?! 6 dxe5 ♕a5+ 7 ♗d2 ♕xe5 8 0-0-0 ♘xe4?? 9 ♕d8+!! ♔xd8 10 ♗g5++ ♔c7** (10...♔e8 11 ♖d8#) **11 ♗d8#**. Very pretty. But I'd like to show you a less well known and even older game, where a top 19th century player, Ignatz von Kolisch, was the victim. **1 e4 e5 2 ♘f3 ♘c6 3 d4 exd4 4 ♘xd4 ♕h4 5 ♘c3 ♗b4 6 ♕d3?! ♘f6 7 ♘xc6 dxc6 8 ♗d2 ♗xc3 9 ♗xc3 ♘xe4 10 ♕d4 ♕e7 11 0-0-0**. Black's risky pawn-grab has worked quite well, but his next move is critical. **11...♕g5+??** (11...♘xc3 12 ♕xg7 ♘xa2+ 13 ♔b1 ♖f8 keeps Black very much in the game) **12 f4! ♕xf4+ 13 ♗d2**. The knight is pinned and the battery on the d-file is loaded.

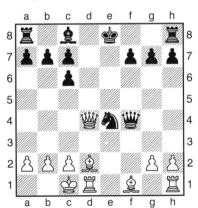

After **13...♕g4 14 ♕d8+! ♔xd8 15 ♗g5++ ♔e8 16 ♖d8#** we have the familiar pattern.

You can have a decoy and a double check without it being a queen sacrifice on the d-file. Here a bishop sacrifice sets up a double check by queen and knight: **1 e4 e5 2 ♘f3 ♘c6 3 ♘c3 f5?!**. This move is risky but not illogical, and White must reply vigorously. **4 d4! fxe4 5 ♘xe5 ♘f6 6 ♗c4 d5?!**. Black appears to have papered over the cracks in his position, but White has seen further. **7 ♘xd5! ♘xd5 8 ♕h5+ g6 9 ♘xg6 ♘f6**.

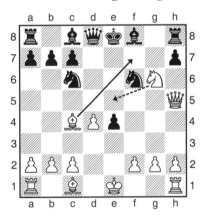

And now what? Any 'normal' move leaves White hopelessly down on material, and a discovered check by the knight is no good because Black simply takes the queen. **10 ♗f7+!**. This is the decoy. **10...♔xf7 11 ♘e5++**. And this is the decisive double check (the knight has much better things to do than grab the rook on h8). It's mate in two more moves: **11...♔e6 12 ♕f7+ ♔d6** (or 12...♔f5 13 g4#) **13 ♘c4#**.

Double Check and Mate

Always double check – it might be... an attack?

As we have just seen, a double check can sometimes force instant mate. But as we shall see in Trap 70, it can also lead nowhere. In this section we look at more complex cases, where a double check leads to an attack that requires deeper calculation to see if it works.

1 c4 e6 2 e4 d5 3 exd5 exd5 4 d4 ♘f6 5 ♘c3 ♘c6 6 ♗g5 dxc4 7 d5?!. Much too optimistic. Rapid development with 7 ♘f3 or even 7 ♗xc4 is preferable. **7...♕e7+ 8 ♕e2?! ♘e5!.** The threat of a knight check on d3 gives White huge problems. **9 ♗xf6?.** White exchanges to give his queen a square on e4, but this does not help. White's best chance is actually for his king to start walking with 9 ♔d2. This sad fact says a lot about how bad his position is! **9...gxf6 10 ♕e4 ♗f5!.**

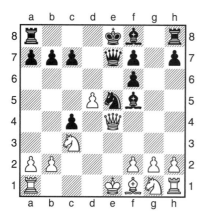

11 ♕xf5 (11 ♕e3 is not a safe square either because of 11...♗h6!) **11...♘f3++!** (only this double check works; 11...♘d3++?? 12 ♔d2 ♗h6+ 13 ♔c2 ♘b4+ 14 ♔d1 lets the king escape) and White is mated after **12 ♔d1 ♕e1+ 13 ♔c2 ♘d4#.**

An even more spectacular sequence catches a king in the centre in the next game:

1 e4 c5 2 ♘f3 g6 3 ♗c4 ♗g7 4 0-0 ♘c6 5 ♖e1 e6 6 ♘c3 d6 7 ♘e2 ♘ge7 8 d4 cxd4 (8...0-0 is OK for Black, as White's knights remain clumsy on e2 and f3) **9 ♘exd4 d5?** (a logical advance, but it fails tactically due to Black's slow development and king in the centre) **10 exd5 ♘xd5** (10...exd5 11 ♗g5 f6 is a better attempt to survive) **11 ♗xd5!? ♕xd5?** (11...♘xd4 12 ♘xd4 0-0 13 ♘xe6 limits White to winning a pawn or two).

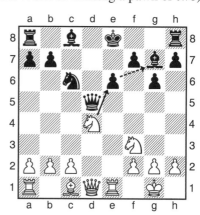

12 ♘xe6!! ♕xd1 13 ♘xg7++ ♔f8 14 ♗h6!! (White is playing purely for mate) **14...♕d8** (desperately trying to cover the mating squares, but the queen will become overloaded) **15 ♘h5+ ♔g8** and now the queen can't guard both f6 and e8, so White has a choice of mates: **16 ♘f6+ ♕xf6 17 ♖e8#** or **16 ♖e8+** (Black resigned here in a recent game played in Portugal) **16...♕xe8 17 ♘f6#.**

Even the greatest of fireworks can fizzle out

The double check is the nuclear weapon of chess tactics. Players are so used to a double check rooting out the enemy king that they forget that sometimes it doesn't work at all. Let's see some examples where players sacrifice too much or damage their own position to make a double check that turns out to be a dud.

1 e4 e5 2 ♘f3 ♘c6 3 ♗b5 f5 4 ♘c3 ♘f6 5 ♕e2 ♘d4 6 ♘xd4 exd4 7 e5 ♘g4. An odd opening has led to a messy position. Now if White calmly plays 8 h3 ♘h6, then either knight retreat (to b1 or d1) gives him a good game. However, he gets sidetracked by a chance to give a double check: **8 e6? c6!**.

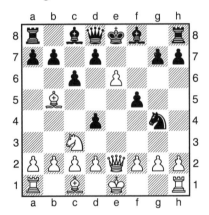

Two white pieces are attacked, and after **9 exd7++ ♔xd7** the black king is quite happy on d7. Black's pieces flood out after **10 ♗d3 ♔c7 11 ♘d1 ♗d6**, creating terrible threats to the jumbled white forces. An old game from Argentina ended **12 ♕f3 ♘e5 13 ♕g3 ♕f6 14 ♗e2 f4 15 ♕b3 ♗e6 16 ♕a4 f3 17 ♗f1 ♖he8 18 ♘e3 dxe3 19 dxe3 fxg2 20 ♗xg2 ♘f3+** and White resigned. Annihilation!

Now we see a game from Greece where Black misses his chance after a successful gambit: **1 d4 d5 2 c4 c6 3 ♘c3 e5 4 cxd5 cxd5 5 dxe5 d4 6 ♘e4 ♕a5+ 7 ♘d2 ♘c6 8 ♘f3 ♗g4 9 ♕b3 ♗b4 10 a3 ♘ge7 11 ♖b1**. Black has very active play. Now 11...♗e6! is good, with the point 12 axb4? ♘xb4 13 ♕d1 ♖c8! 14 ♘xd4 ♘f5! and invading on c2. Instead **11...♗f5?** is based on an idea with a double check, but it's wrong.

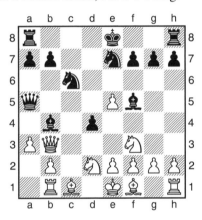

12 axb4! (improving over the other 'move' played in this position, which apparently was... to resign! See Trap 99 for more on this type of error) **12...♘xb4 13 e4!** (the only way to save the rook) **13...dxe3 14 ♘c4!** and now Black has a choice of double checks that achieve nothing: **14...♘d3++** (or 14...♘c2++ 15 ♔e2) **15 ♔d1 ♘xf2+ 16 ♔e2 ♕a6 17 ♔xe3! ♘g4+ 18 ♔f4! ♘d5+ 19 ♔g3** (finally reaching safety after a stunning king-walk) **19...0-0 20 ♘d6** and, with most of Black's pieces attacked, White is winning.

TRAP 71 — Geometry: Decoy and Knight Fork

Picture the fork and work out how to make it happen

Certain pairs of squares are two knight moves apart: d1 and h1 is one such pair, as is d8 and e5. So what? If we have a knight that can get to a square that attacks them both, and can force our opponent's pieces to those squares, we have the makings of a killing knight fork. Let's see how it's done.

1 e4 c6 2 ♘c3 d5 3 ♘f3 ♘f6 4 e5 ♘e4 5 ♘xe4 dxe4 6 ♘g5 ♕d5 7 d3 exd3 8 ♗xd3 ♕xe5+ 9 ♗e3. White has sacrificed a pawn for a big lead in development. There is also a potential tactic: a knight on f7 would fork pieces on d8 and e5. That sounds very abstract, as so far there is just a piece on e5 and f7 is defended, but after Black's next move it suddenly becomes real. **9...g6?** (9...h6 10 ♘f3 ♕c7 is probably best, but Black has a hard defence ahead of him).

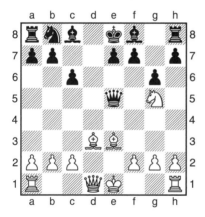

10 ♗c4!. By hitting f7, White opens the d-file with gain of time. After **10...e6**, **11 ♕d8+!** drags the king into position to be forked. After **11...♔xd8 12 ♘xf7+ ♔e8 13 ♘xe5** White has won back his pawn while staying ahead in development and leaving Black with weak pawns. His advantage is huge. The fact that Black actually went on to draw this grandmaster game (between

Rossolimo and Szabo) goes to show how vital it is to fight hard for every half-point.

This idea doesn't have to involve a dramatic queen sacrifice. An exchange of queens can also set up a knight fork of king and rook in the corner. After **1 ♘f3 d5 2 g3 c5 3 ♗g2 ♘c6 4 d4 ♘f6 5 0-0 e6 6 c4 dxc4 7 ♘e5** Black needs to be careful, as his most obvious moves have serious drawbacks. 7...cxd4?? 8 ♘xc6 bxc6 9 ♗xc6+ is a disaster for Black, while 7...♘xe5 8 dxe5 ♕xd1 9 ♖xd1 ♘d5 10 ♘c3 leaves him under heavy pressure. Can you see why **7...♘xd4??** loses?

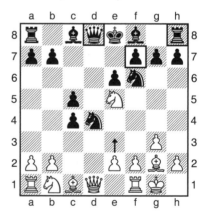

After **8 e3!** Black can't avoid a knight fork on f7. **8...♘f5** (8...♘c6 is no improvement due to 9 ♗xc6+! bxc6 10 ♕xd8+) **9 ♕xd8+ ♔xd8 10 ♘xf7+** and after ♘xh8 White wins a rook. Although Black can trap the knight in the corner, White has a decisive material plus.

Until the bishop has moved, it's just a silly pawn advance

The fianchetto is a standard way to develop a bishop. But moving the knight's pawn leaves the rook briefly exposed to attack. If we are too busy fighting for the centre to complete the fianchetto, that might come back to haunt us.

An example from a recent Indian championship will make the theme clear. **1 c4 ♘f6 2 g3 c6 3 d4 d5** and with **4 ♘d2?!** White wants to play it safe by not allowing Black to grab the pawn on c4. However, this move has the opposite effect. **4...dxc4! 5 ♘xc4?? ♕d5!**.

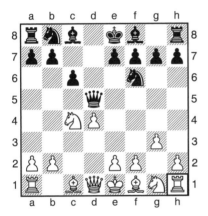

While a tragedy for the player who allowed this move, it illustrates our theme perfectly. The queen forks the rook and knight from a square that the bishop would have covered – *if only it were already on g2*. **6 e4** is a creative attempt to get some play against the black king, but after **6...♕xe4+ 7 ♕e2 ♕xh1 8 ♘d6+ ♔d7 9 ♘xf7 ♕xg1** White has lost too much material and the invading black queen also pins the f1-bishop. **10 ♗g5 ♕xh2** changes little, as the queen still prevents ♗h3+.

Now let's see a game from a qualifying event for a Soviet championship where Black

had to work harder to make this theme come true. **1 d4 d5 2 c4 dxc4 3 ♘f3 ♗g4 4 ♘e5 ♗h5 5 ♘c3 ♘f6 6 ♗g5 c6 7 ♘xc4**. We see loose pieces on c4 and g5, but for now Black has no way to attack them both. **7...♘bd7 8 g3**. There's a third loose piece on h1. **8...♘b6 9 ♘a5?!**. Loose pieces everywhere... but Black still needs a way to attack them. With **9...♘bd5!** he hits a5 directly and prepares to remove the defender of the d5-square.

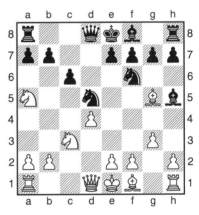

10 ♘b3??. Missing the danger. White can make a fight of it by 10 ♘xb7 ♘xc3 11 bxc3 ♕d5 12 ♖g1 ♕xg5 13 ♗g2. **10...♘xc3 11 bxc3 ♕d5!**. And here we have a double attack. After **12 ♗xf6 ♕xh1 13 ♗e5 e6 14 ♕d2 f6 15 ♗f4 0-0-0** White is knight for rook down, and can do little more than thrash around. But thrash around he did, and was eventually rewarded with a horrible blunder by Black and an unlikely victory. Never relax until the point is scored!

TRAP 73 The Exposed Bishop

Look out for the ♕a4+ fork, even if it doesn't win on the spot

In several openings it is standard for Black to put his bishop on b4. There are all sorts of good reasons for this, but the bishop can be in danger on this square. It might be attacked by pawns, or sometimes lost due to a queen check, as we are about to see.

1 d4 ♘f6 2 c4 e6 3 ♘c3 ♗b4 4 ♘f3 b6 5 ♗g5 ♗b7 6 ♘d2 h6 7 ♗h4 d6??. This is a shockingly common error in positions of this type. Black wants to play flexibly and keep his options open (rather than castling first), but misses a simple tactic. **8 ♕a4+ ♘c6**. So Black has everything covered, right? Sadly, Black is now pinned to death:

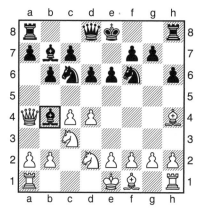

After **9 d5 ♗xc3 10 bxc3** Black has saved his bishop, but there is no rescue for his poor knight. 10...exd5 11 cxd5 ♘xd5?? is no go because this knight is pinned too, while 10...g5 fails to break that pin in time as 11 dxc6 gxh4 12 cxb7+ wins the house.

With that in mind, let's see a supergrandmaster game on a similar theme. **1 ♘f3 ♘f6 2 c4 c5 3 ♘c3 ♘c6 4 e3 e6 5 d4 d5 6 cxd5 exd5 7 ♗e2 cxd4 8 exd4**. Not much is happening so far, but with his next couple of moves, Timman (one of the best Western players of the 1980s and 1990s) unwisely provokes Tal (World Champion 1960-1 and an attacking genius). **8...♘e4?! 9 0-0 ♗b4?**. The exposed bishop appears.

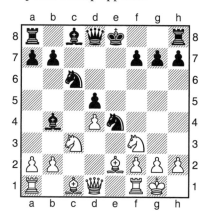

10 ♘xe4 dxe4 11 d5 knocks away the bishop's defender. Of course, with his own knight on f3 also attacked, White won't be winning a piece, but he has worked out he will make other gains. **11...exf3 12 ♗xf3 ♘e5** (12...0-0 13 dxc6 leaves Black a pawn down) **13 ♕a4+**. Here is the familiar queen fork. After **13...♕d7 14 ♕xb4 ♘xf3+ 15 gxf3 ♕xd5** the dust has cleared. Black is behind in development and his king is caught in the centre. That's all an attacking genius needs, and Tal won after **16 ♗f4 ♗e6 17 ♖fe1 a5 18 ♕a3 ♖c8? 19 ♖ad1 ♕c5 20 ♖c1! 1-0**. Ouch! 20...♕xa3 21 ♖xc8+ ♔e7 22 ♖c7+! followed by bxa3 leaves White a rook up.

TRAP 74   A Horrible Discovery

Checks? No. Captures? No. Threats? Uh-huh.

After just a little experience, we get accustomed to spotting 'violent' tactical ideas, such as checks and captures. But 'quiet' moves are harder to see, even when they are mighty powerful. Our theme in this Trap is a bishop discovering an attack on a queen, but all the bishop does itself is threaten a pawn. However, this second attack proves decisive.

1 e4 c6 2 ♘f3 d5 3 exd5 cxd5 4 ♘e5 ♘c6 5 d4 ♕b6 6 c3 ♘xe5 7 dxe5 e6 8 ♗d3 ♗d7 9 ♕e2 d4?!. Black should develop instead. **10 0-0 ♘e7 11 cxd4 ♕xd4 12 ♘c3 a6 13 ♖d1 ♘c6? 14 ♗g6!!**. White has a number of good moves here, but directly targeting the king makes a lot of sense!

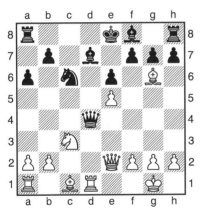

14...♕xe5. Other queen moves are answered in the same way. **15 ♗xf7+ ♔e7** (15...♔xf7 16 ♖xd7+ will leave Black at least a pawn down and under attack) **16 ♗h5! ♕xe2?**. This allows a snap mate, but 16...g6 17 ♘e4 intending ♗g5+ gives White a decisive attack. **17 ♗g5#**. Very neat! This happened in a 2018 game in an under-17 event, so is one of the few games in this book between players born in the 21st century!

1 e4 c6 2 d4 d5 3 e5 ♗f5 4 ♘c3 e6 5 g4 ♗g6 6 ♘ge2 ♘e7 7 ♘f4 h5?!. Black should focus more on development. 7...c5 and 7...♘d7 are better ways to face White's aggressive advances. **8 ♘xg6 ♘xg6 9 gxh5 ♘h4 10 ♕g4 ♘f5 11 ♗d3 ♘h6 12 ♗xh6 ♖xh6 13 f4 ♕b6 14 0-0-0 ♕xd4?**. Black will come under attack anyway, but this allows a direct blow.

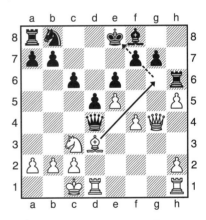

15 ♗g6!. By pinning the f7-pawn and blocking the h6-rook, White threatens ♕xe6+. **15...♕e3+ 16 ♔b1 fxg6** (16...♔e7 17 ♖he1 ♕b6 18 f5 gives White an unstoppable attack) **17 ♕xe6+ ♗e7** (or 17...♔d8 18 ♘xd5 cxd5 19 ♕xd5+) **18 hxg6** leaves Black with no good answer to White's many threats, which include ♕f7+.

Fantasy Caro: The Main Trap

You'd need a great sense of danger to dodge this bullet

This whole section is devoted to an elaborate trap in the Caro-Kann. At first it looks like Black has played a clever combination with a pawn promotion, but it turns out that White has seen further.

After **1 e4 c6 2 d4 d5** the move **3 f3** is called the Fantasy Variation. It is a rare but logical reply to the Caro-Kann – White seeks to keep his *two-abreast pawn-centre* on d4 and e4. One of the main points behind it is that one of Black's most logical responses leads directly to disaster for him. **3...dxe4 4 fxe4 e5**. Black hits back in the centre and seeks to expose White's king – what could possibly be wrong with that? Well, nothing much, but White has a good reply: **5 ②f3! exd4?!**. This is at the very least risky. 5...≗e6 and 5...≗g4 are the normal moves, leading to a lively fight. **6 ≗c4**.

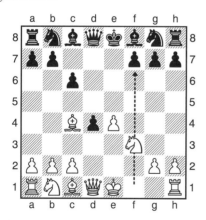

This is the problem. White has a lead in development and threats against the f7-square. Note the *half-open* f-file. **6...≗b4+?** (6...≗g4?? allows a typical tactic that we know from Trap 11: 7 ≗xf7+ ≗xf7 8 ②e5+) **7 c3! dxc3?**. This loses tactically, but otherwise Black is simply being pushed

backwards. 7...≗a5 is the only move to keep any chances alive. **8 ≗xf7+ ≗xf7** (8...≗e7 9 ≝b3 is hopeless for Black because 9...c2+ 10 ≝xb4+ comes with check – material will be level, but the black king is terribly exposed) **9 ≝xd8 cxb2+ 10 ≗e2 bxa1≝**.

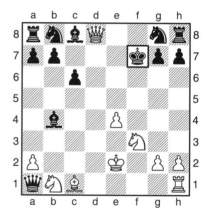

This was Black's idea – he has regained his sacrificed queen, keeping an extra rook and bishop(!). However, it is White to play and he has a forced mate: **11 ②g5+ ≗g6 12 ≝e8+ ≗h6** (or 12...≗f6 13 ≖f1+) **13 ②e6+ g5 14 ≗xg5#**.

This idea has won more than 40 games for White, though of course in most cases Black has not played all the way to mate. The victims include some rather strong players. This is not surprising: Black's moves appear very logical, and it would be almost impossible to see the mating line when deciding on Black's 5th and 6th moves. And after that point, Black only has bad options.

TRAP 76

Mating with ♘xf7

A clear and ever-present danger

One of the standard reasons for a ♘xf7 sacrifice is to smash through with the queen on e6 and mate the black king. First we have a basic example, where Black spotted the problem first time around but allowed it five moves later. Our second example shows a far less ordinary follow-up.

1 e4 c6 2 d4 d5 3 ♘c3 dxe4 4 ♘xe4 ♘d7 5 ♘g5 ♘gf6 6 ♗c4 e6. Black intends to move his king's bishop, castle and then continue normal development. White's next move throws a spanner in the works. **7 ♕e2** threatens ♘xf7, and many games in this opening line have ended with a quick attack based on that move. If Black is aware of the danger, then he can defend against it by altering his development plan. **7...♘b6 8 ♗b3 h6** (not the greedy 8...♕xd4? since White replies 9 ♘1f3 followed by ♘e5, and smashes through on f7) **9 ♘5f3 a5 10 c3 c5 11 dxc5 ♗xc5 12 ♘e5 ♘bd7??**.

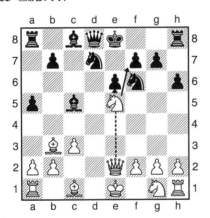

Black forgets about White's sacrifice on f7, having carefully avoided it five moves earlier. **13 ♘xf7! ♔xf7 14 ♕xe6+ ♔g6** (or 14...♔f8 15 ♕f7#) **15 ♗c2+** (of several ways to mate, this is quickest) **15...♔h5 16 ♕h3#**.

Sometimes the follow-up to a ♘xf7 sacrifice is more subtle: **1 e4 c6 2 d4 d5 3 ♘c3 dxe4 4 ♘xe4 ♘d7 5 ♗d3 ♘df6 6 ♘g5 ♗g4 7 ♘1f3**. At this point ♘xf7 is not threatened, so Black takes the opportunity to force the knight to retreat: **7...h6?? 8 ♘xf7!!**. But it doesn't retreat, as the weakened g6-square changes everything. **8...♗xf3** (8...♔xf7 9 ♘e5+ is of course terrible for Black – it's Trap 11 again).

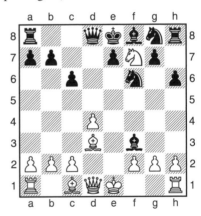

9 ♗g6!!. Rather than saving his pieces, White threatens mate. (Instead, 9 ♘xd8? ♗xd1 is at least OK for Black, while 9 ♘e5? ♕a5+ 10 ♗d2 ♕xe5+ 11 dxe5 ♗xd1 12 ♖xd1 is a crazy line that Black may survive – ask your computer for details!) **9...♗xd1** allows **10 ♘e5#**, while the only way to play on is **9...♕a5+**, but **10 ♗d2** followed by ♘xh8+ will leave Black hopelessly down on material.

TRAP 77

Crashing Through on f7 and e6

A rook stuck in the enemy king's throat

As we have just seen, a sacrifice on f7 is a good way to rip the defences from a king, especially when we can follow up by smashing through on the e6-square. This is true even when there is no instant win – pieces lodged in the heart of the enemy position can form the spearhead of a slower attack. This is a general theme rather than a specific opening trap, but the two examples that follow show how effective it can be. It is actually Black attacking in these games, so the key squares here are in fact f2 and e3.

1 d4 ♘f6 2 c4 e5 3 dxe5 ♘g4 4 ♘f3 ♗c5 5 e3 ♘c6 6 ♗d2 0-0 7 ♗d3 ♖e8 8 ♗c3 d6! (White's idea was 8...♘gxe5 9 ♘xe5 ♘xe5 10 ♗xh7+ ♔xh7 11 ♕h5+ ♔g8 12 ♗xe5, as in Trap 55) **9 exd6?.** Opening lines for Black is fatal. White should have let Black recapture the pawn and settled in for a tough battle.

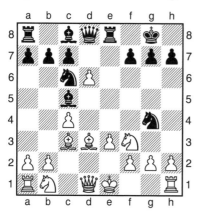

9...♘xf2! 10 ♔xf2 ♖xe3 11 ♔f1 ♕xd6 12 ♗e2 ♕e7 happened in a game in Greece. Black has too many threats, such as ...♗f5 followed by ...♖d8 and ...♖xf3+!. White's extra piece provides little comfort, and after **13 a3 ♗f5 14 b4 ♖d8 15 ♘bd2 ♖xe2 16 ♕xe2 ♗d3** White could have resigned.

In our next example, the position is different but the story is similar: **1 d4 ♘f6 2 c4 c5 3 ♘f3 cxd4 4 ♘xd4 e5 5 ♘b5 d5 6 cxd5**

♗c5 7 ♘5c3 0-0. Again, Black has played an aggressive gambit – this one is named the Vaganian Gambit, after an Armenian grandmaster. **8 g3 ♘g4 9 e3 f5 10 ♗g2?! f4 11 h3?.** "Please punch me in the face." **11...♘xf2! 12 ♔xf2 fxe3++ 13 ♔e1 ♖f2.**

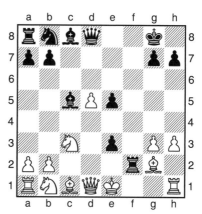

Black has a powerful attack in return for the piece, as the white king will find no safety. **14 ♖g1?** (14 ♘e4 keeps some hope of survival in a wild battle, but perhaps White was still hoping to consolidate) **14...♕f8 15 ♕d3 ♘a6 16 a3 ♗f5 17 ♗e4 ♗xe4 18 ♕xe4 ♗d4 19 ♗xe3? ♘c5 20 ♗xd4 exd4 21 ♕xd4 ♖e8+ 22 ♔d1 ♕f3+** and White resigned, as he will be mated. Who was Black in this beautiful game? An 11-year-old Hungarian girl: Judit Polgar.

Great Queen Traps of Our Time

Even the queen needs an exit plan

Sometimes the queen can be in more serious danger than it seems. We are used to the queen's great mobility making it a very hard piece to trap unless it is truly boxed in. Here we shall see two cases where a queen suddenly finds that all its escape-routes are unexpectedly closed off.

1 e4 e6 2 d4 d5 3 ♘c3 ♘f6 4 ♗g5 ♗e7 5 e5 ♘e4 6 ♘xe4 ♗xg5 7 ♘xg5 ♕xg5 8 ♘f3 ♕e7 9 ♗d3 ♕b4+ 10 ♕d2 ♕xb2 11 0-0. Black has played a little riskily, but with care he should get a playable game. **11...h6??**. Black prevents the annoying move ♕g5, but it was already time to head for the emergency exit with 11...♕a3, making sure the queen lives to fight another day. (11...0-0?? allows a different queen-trap: 12 ♗xh7+ ♔xh7 13 ♕d3+ g6 14 ♖fb1.) **12 a4!**.

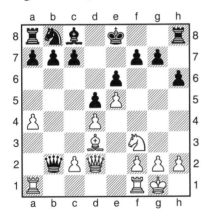

It seems hard to believe, but the queen is trapped! 13 ♖fb1 is a threat, and **12...♕b6 13 ♖fb1 ♕c6** (there's nowhere else) **14 ♗b5** pins and wins the queen.

Here is a game where the queen appears to have plenty of space midboard, but it is an illusion: **1 g3 d5 2 ♗g2 e6 3 d3 ♗c5 4 ♘d2 ♘f6 5 ♘gf3? ♗xf2+! 6 ♔xf2 ♘g4+ 7 ♔g1 ♘e3 8 ♕e1 ♘xc2 9 ♕d1 ♘xa1 10**

♘f1 ♕f6?! 11 d4 ♕g6?! 12 ♗f4 ♕c2 13 ♕xa1 ♕xe2 14 ♘1d2. The play in this game, from a French junior tournament, has not been very accurate. First White allowed the idea from Trap 16. Then Black decided to play only with his queen instead of developing his other pieces.

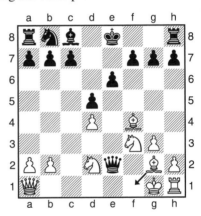

With **14...♘c6??** he finally developed another piece, when he should have been rescuing his queen (with 14...♕b5 or 14...♕a6). **15 ♗f1!**. Backward bishop moves can be hard to spot, and it must have been a horrible realization for Black that his 'active' queen has no safe squares at all. White wins.

So judge carefully when you need to evacuate the queen. Not too early: a queen in the middle of the enemy forces can prove mighty powerful, and prevent the opponent's best plans. But don't wait too long to evacuate her majesty, or you might find it is too late.

TRAP 79 — More Queen Traps

Locked up abroad: Queen edition

Queens can become trapped in all parts of the board and in many ways. We may not even have to *take* the queen – merely *imprisoning* it can let us launch an attack in another part of the board.

1 e4 c5 2 ♘c3 ♘c6 3 g3 g6 4 ♗g2 ♗g7 5 d3 d6 6 ♗e3 e5 7 ♕d2 ♘ge7 8 ♗h6 0-0 9 h4. White is attacking, and his queen seems extremely unlikely to be trapped. Yet with the little pawn move **9...f6!?** Black has precisely that in mind. White should now exchange bishops on g7, since **10 h5??** falls straight into Black's trap. **10...♗xh6 11 ♕xh6 g5!** walls the queen in.

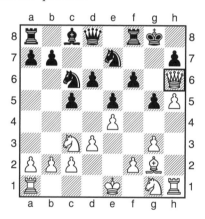

White can't do anything against the simple plan of ...♔h8 and ...♘g8. After **12 ♘d5 ♘xd5 13 exd5 ♘d4** he threatens both ...♘f5 and ...♘xc2+. This trap was first sprung by Grandmaster Semion Furman, who was for many years the coach of Anatoly Karpov (World Champion 1975-85). The idea of trapping the queen on h6 by playing ...g5 is a key defensive theme in several openings where Black fianchettoes his king's bishop.

Let's see another example where a queen unwisely strays into foreign territory. **1 d4 e6 2 c4 c5 3 ♘f3 cxd4 4 ♘xd4 a6 5 g3 ♕c7 6 ♘d2 ♗b4 7 ♕b3 ♘c6?**. Black was probably happy with this move, exploiting the *Uncompleted Fianchetto* (Trap 72) on White's kingside. But when using this idea, it is important to check that the queen can either escape or take a lot of enemy pieces down with it. However, after **8 ♘xc6! ♕xc6?** (Black should bail out with 8...♗xd2+ 9 ♗xd2 ♕xc6, but Black has exchanged off his best pieces and given White a space advantage) **9 ♕xb4! ♕xh1 10 ♘f3**, this is not so.

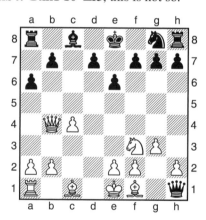

White threatens to win the queen for a rook (by ♗e3, 0-0-0 and ♗h3) or to create mate threats against the black king. After **10...b5** (hoping to free the queen by ...♗b7 and ...♗xf3) **11 b3! ♗b7 12 ♗a3!**, a master-level game in Yugoslavia ended brutally with **12...0-0-0** (12...♗xf3? 13 ♕f8#) **13 cxb5 ♘e7 14 ♖c1+ ♘c6 15 bxa6 ♗xa6 16 ♕b6 1-0**, due to 16...♗b7 17 ♗d6 and ♕c7#.

Rook Cornered by Bishops

When diagonals are long and files are short

The rook is a mighty powerful piece – second only to the queen. But that's when it has room to breathe. At the start of the game it is boxed in the corner, and takes a long time to come into play. Until ranks and files open up, the rook is vulnerable to diagonal attack, and two bishops working together can easily trap it. This can happen with no obvious blunders being made.

After **1 d4 d5 2 c4 c6 3 cxd5 cxd5 4 ♘c3 ♘f6 5 ♗f4 ♗f5 6 e3 ♘c6 7 ♘f3 e6 8 ♗b5 ♖c8 9 ♘e5** the position looks very simple, and Black's next move, **9...♗e7??**, appears completely safe at first sight. But it loses because White can now snare a black rook: **10 ♘xc6! bxc6 11 ♗a6.**

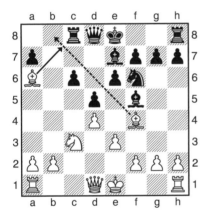

That's that – the rook is toast. **11...♖a8 12 ♗b7** is the end of the road for the poor rook.

This rook trap occurs in all sorts of openings and central structures. Here is another instance: **1 d4 d5 2 ♘f3 e6 3 c4 c5 4 e3 cxd4 5 exd4 ♘f6 6 ♘c3 ♘c6 7 ♗d3 ♗e7 8 0-0 0-0 9 a3 b6.** This move ends up haunting Black, but it is not an error in itself. With **10 cxd5 exd5** (Black chooses not to head for an IQP – see Trap 83 – by playing 10...♘xd5) **11 h3** White rules out ...♗g4 and makes it hard for Black to find a good home for his queen's bishop.

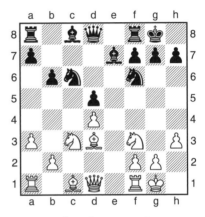

11...h6 12 ♗f4 ♗e6 (12...♗b7 leaves the bishop doing little as the d5-pawn blocks its diagonal) **13 ♖c1 ♖c8??**.

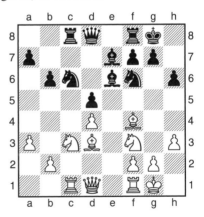

An obvious developing move, but a fatal blunder. **14 ♗a6!** traps the rook. It looks like Black really set himself up for this, but each of his moves seemed natural and logical.

TRAP 81 — Amazing Pawn Promotions

The humble pawn is the star of these shows

Pawns promoting in the opening? Seriously? Yes, this can and does happen. There are even some 'four queens' opening lines where both sides promote. Our examples in this section feature surprising promotion tricks. In the first, an *underpromotion* to a knight helps win the enemy queen. The second is basically a queen swap – White loses his queen, but it is reborn, taking a black rook in the process.

One of the best-known opening traps features a promotion to a *knight*: **1 d4 d5 2 c4 e5** (this is the Albin Counter-Gambit) **3 dxe5 d4 4 e3?!** (White tries to eliminate Black's central d4-pawn straight away – which would be a great idea if it didn't fail tactically!) **4...♗b4+! 5 ♗d2 dxe3!**. This appears to lose a piece, but the key point is seen after **6 ♗xb4?? exf2+ 7 ♔e2**.

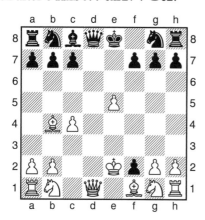

Now 7...fxg1♕? is no good because White exchanges queens on d8 before taking on g1, while 7...♗g4+?? 8 ♘f3 gives Black nothing. But **7...fxg1♘+!!** promotes *with check* so Black wins the white queen after **8 ♖xg1** (or 8 ♔e1 ♕h4+) **8...♗g4+**.

The next promotion idea is a more standard way to exploit an exposed king, but still very surprising if you haven't seen the basic

pattern before. **1 e4 e5 2 ♘f3 ♘c6 3 c3 f5** (a reversed Vienna Gambit, but 3...♘f6 is simpler) **4 exf5 e4 5 ♘d4!**. White makes use of the central square his third move covered and has a cunning trick in mind if Black exchanges. **5...♘xd4? 6 ♕h5+! g6 7 fxg6! ♘f6** (7...♗g7 lets White regain his piece and keep a couple of extra pawns) **8 g7+!**.

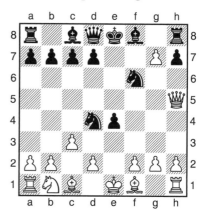

The point: otherwise White is losing. This tactic basically swaps the queen on h5 for one on h8, but picks up a rook along the way! **8...♘xh5 9 gxh8♕ ♘c2+ 10 ♔d1**. This happened in an old game where Ben Finegold was White. Nowadays you'll often find him commenting on major events at Saint Louis. After **10...♘xa1 11 ♕e5+ ♕e7 12 ♕xh5+** the dust has settled and White will round up the trapped knight on a1.

In the Footsteps of Perlis

Putting an amazing promotion theme to work

This stunning promotion idea is based on a pawn attacking a knight on its starting square. If the knight weren't there at all, the pawn could be stopped. But as it is, the pawn threatens to promote on two different squares, and they can't both be covered.

The classic example on this theme is an old game between Schlechter and Perlis. Here is a more modern game that features the idea in even clearer form: **1 d4 ♘f6 2 ♗g5 ♘e4 3 ♗f4 c5 4 c3 ♕b6 5 ♕b3?! cxd4! 6 ♕xb6 axb6**. The opening has not gone well for White so far. The a-file is very useful for Black. Now 7 cxd4 ♘c6 leaves White unable to save his d4-pawn because of 8 ♘f3 ♘b4! 9 ♘a3? ♖xa3!. So White tries to eliminate the b8-knight before taking on d4, but only digs a deeper hole for himself: **7 ♗xb8 dxc3! 8 ♗e5??**. White desperately tries to defend b2. Instead 8 ♘xc3 ♘xc3 9 bxc3 ♖xb8 leaves Black a pawn up for nothing.

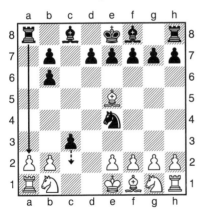

8...♖xa2!!. This brilliant move was played by Joe Gallagher in 1990. After **9 ♖xa2 c2** the pawn promotes on b1 or c1. White can defend either one of these squares, but not both of them at once.

Now let's see a game where this idea lay more deeply hidden, but was just as important. **1 d4 d5 2 c4 c6 3 ♘c3 ♘f6 4 e3 ♗g4 5 ♕b3 ♕b6 6 h3 ♗f5 7 g4! ♕xb3?! 8 axb3 ♗c2 9 g5**. Amazingly, Black already has a serious problem. He can't save his d5-pawn, and it's all because of the promotion trick! **9...♘e4** (9...♘fd7 10 cxd5 ♗xb3 holds out more hope) **10 cxd5!**.

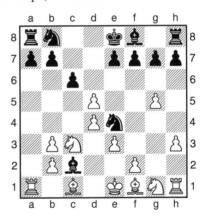

10...♘xc3. Black wants to insert the exchange of knights before recapturing on d5, but we already know why that isn't going to happen! **11 dxc6! ♗e4?** (but 11...♘xc6 12 bxc3 ♗xb3 13 e4 leaves Black facing a huge swathe of advancing pawns) **12 ♖xa7!! ♖xa7 13 c7** and the pawn promotes.

So remember: a knight on *any* edge of the board is highly vulnerable to attack by a pawn, as it has fewer squares it can go to. This is an endgame theme too!

The IQP Trap

Its sudden advance can open the floodgates

This wonderfully logical tactic tends to occur when White has an isolated queen's pawn (IQP) and very active pieces. IQPs can occur from many openings, such as the Nimzo-Indian and Semi-Tarrasch in addition to the Caro-Kann in our main example.

As the idea involves several steps, let's look first of all at a simpler position where White just needs to play the final tactic of the sequence. **1 e4 e5 2 ♘f3 ♘f6 3 ♘xe5 d6 4 ♘f3 ♘xe4 5 ♘c3 ♘f6 6 d4 d5 7 ♗d3 ♗e7 8 0-0 0-0 9 h3 ♘c6 10 ♖e1 ♘b4 11 ♗g5 ♘xd3 12 ♕xd3 g6??**. Black is dreaming of playing ...♗f5, but this move creates a fatal weakness.

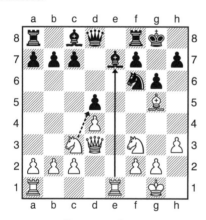

13 ♖xe7! ♕xe7 14 ♘xd5. White's exchange sacrifice (rook for bishop) has led to a deadly pin, which the knight immediately exploits. Black will lose the f6-knight and be hopelessly down on material.

OK, so there was no IQP there, but bear with me. All will be revealed. After **1 e4 c6 2 c4 d5 3 exd5 cxd5 4 cxd5 ♘f6 5 ♘c3 ♘xd5 6 ♘f3 e6 7 d4 ♘c6 8 ♗d3 ♗e7 9 0-0 0-0 10 ♖e1 ♘f6 11 a3 b6 12 ♗c2 ♗b7 13 ♕d3** everything is ready for the full IQP trap to be sprung. However, it is not at all

obvious unless you have seen the idea before, which explains why so many players have fallen right into it. The hundreds of victims include grandmasters and world champions. **13...♖c8? 14 d5!**.

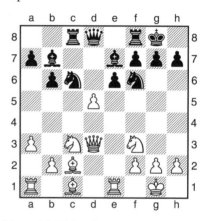

14...exd5. This allows White's main idea, but Black has no good options here. 14...♘a5 15 ♗g5 ♖xc3 16 ♕xc3 ♕xd5 leaves him materially down. **15 ♗g5!**. The threat is ♗xf6 followed by mate on h7. **15...g6**. This is the only defence (as 15...♘e4 16 ♘xe4 dxe4 17 ♕xe4 g6 18 ♕h4 ♗xg5 19 ♘xg5 h5 20 ♗xg6! fxg6 21 ♕c4+ gives White a winning attack), but we already know what happens next! **16 ♖xe7! ♕xe7** (16...♘xe7 allows 17 ♗xf6) **17 ♘xd5** and Black must give up his queen with **17...♕xd5 18 ♗xe7 ♘cxe7**, but White should win the game comfortably.

We should note that an IQP is definitely not an advantage in itself. It can also be a weakness. It all depends on the position.

Overwhelming Development

Defeated by sheer weight of numbers

Sometimes a position disintegrates not because of a specific tactic, but because the opponent has a huge advantage in development. The attacking pieces pile in and the defences are routed.

1 e4 c5 2 d4 cxd4 3 c3 dxc3 4 ♘xc3 ♘c6 5 ♘f3 d6 6 ♗c4 e6 7 0-0 ♗e7 8 ♕e2 ♘f6 9 ♖d1 is one of the standard positions in the Morra Gambit. By creating a pin on the d-file, White now threatens e5, an idea Black should not ignore. Let's see why. **9...0-0?! 10 e5 ♘e8 11 exd6 ♗xd6**. Is this just an exchange of pawns? No, because Black's bishop is pinned and White can crank up the pressure immediately. **12 ♘b5 ♕e7 13 ♗g5!**. A key move, and a typical one. As soon as a development advantage starts growing, it can quickly snowball. **13...f6**. Now the e6-pawn is weak, and pinned too. **14 ♗e3**.

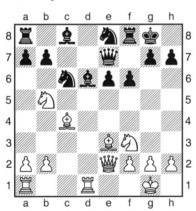

White threatens 15 ♖xd6! ♘xd6 16 ♗c5. **14...♗b8?** (14...b6 and 14...♗c5 are better defences) **15 ♖ac1** (now the threat is 16 ♗c5 ♕xc5 17 ♗xe6+) **15...b6 16 ♗b3 ♗b7 17 ♗c5 bxc5 18 ♗xe6+ ♔h8 19 ♖d7** and Black resigned in a game played many years ago in Germany. His queen is trapped.

In our next example, Black plays a tactical trick, but it leaves White's pieces much too active. After **1 e4 c5 2 ♘f3 d6 3 d4 cxd4 4 ♘xd4 ♘f6 5 ♘c3 a6 6 ♗c4 e6**, Anand once told me about a cunning idea behind the move **7 0-0!?**. White is tempting Black into playing **7...♘xe4?** based on the pawn fork **8 ♘xe4 d5**. Black will regain his piece, but allows White a large development advantage. After **9 ♗g5!** it was obvious to Anand that Black would not survive, but let's see some variations. (After all, we are not all world champions...)

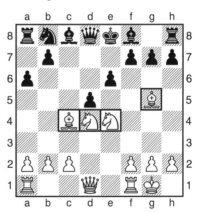

9...♕d7 10 ♕h5!? dxc4 11 ♖ad1 and there is no defence to White's many threats, which include 12 ♘xe6 ♕xe6 13 ♖d8#. After **9...♗e7**, one good solution is **10 ♗xe7 ♕xe7 11 ♗xd5 exd5 12 ♘c3**, when Black must either allow ♖e1+ and a deadly attack, or else let White win a pawn on d5. This trap has since claimed a number of victims.

TRAP 85

A Stab in the Heart

A knight on e3 is hard to foresee

I have to admit that the idea we are about to look at doesn't crop up too often, but it is so beautiful that I felt I had to include it anyway. If nothing else, it reminds us that we should always use our imagination and be on the lookout for astonishing moves.

1 d4 ♘f6 2 c4 g6 3 ♘c3 d5 4 ♕b3 dxc4 5 ♕xc4 ♗e6 6 ♕b5+ ♘c6 7 ♘f3 ♘d5 8 e4 a6 9 ♕b3?. This move looks very natural, and it is difficult to believe that it puts the queen in grave danger. (White should play 9 ♕a4 or 9 ♕e2 instead.) The amazing move **9...♘e3!!** is the point – and also our theme in this section.

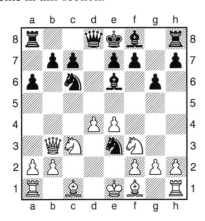

The knight dives into the heart of White's position, sowing chaos and confusion. It looks like an absurd square for a knight, but White's problems with his queen are more important. Now 10 ♕a3? ♘c2+ is a simple fork, as is 10 ♕xb7 ♘a5 11 ♕b4? ♘c2+. Amazingly, 10 d5 ♘a5! 11 ♕a4+ ♗d7! 12 ♕xa5 ♘c2+ 13 ♔d1 b6! leaves the white queen trapped! And after **10 ♘d5 ♘xd5 11 exd5 ♕xd5 12 ♕xb7 ♕e4+! 13 ♗e3 ♖a7** the queen is finally trapped in a most unusual manner. This all happened in an Italian game played by mail.

Let's see another example – taken from a German championship – where the knight plunges into the same square. The ideas are different, but it is just as unexpected. **1 d4 ♘f6 2 c4 e6 3 ♘f3 b6 4 g3 ♗a6 5 ♘bd2 c5 6 e4 cxd4 7 ♗g2 ♘c6 8 e5 ♘g4 9 0-0 ♖b8 10 ♖e1 ♗c5.**

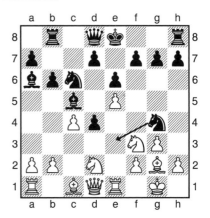

A battle is raging in the centre. Now 11 ♘e4 would give White a good game, but instead he played **11 h3?**. He must have imagined he was forcing the knight back, and worked out that 11...♘xf2? 12 ♔xf2 d3+ 13 ♔f1 is not a problem for White. But after **11...♘e3!!** White resigned. After **12 fxe3** (12 ♕a4 ♘xg2 and 13 ♕xa6 doesn't save White because Black can take the rook on e1, while 13 ♔xg2 ♗b7 leaves Black dominating the board) **12...dxe3** he has to move his king to avoid a deadly discovered check. Then capturing on d2 will leave White a pawn down with a terrible position.

TRAP 86

Castle the Intruder Away

An elegant way to deal with an unwelcome guest

We previously saw (in Trap 27) an idea where White castled queenside with a black rook on b2. There is another possibility for a shocking castling move that attacks an intruding piece when a black knight appears on d2 (or a white knight on d7).

After **1 e4 d5 2 exd5 ♕xd5 3 d4 e5 4 ♘f3 ♗g4 5 ♗e2 e4 6 ♘e5** (6 ♘c3! ♗b4 7 ♘d2 is best) **6...♗xe2 7 ♕xe2 ♕xd4** White should make a gambit of it by playing 8 ♗f4. Instead, trying to get the pawn back with **8 ♕b5+? ♘d7 9 ♘xd7?** runs into problems. White sees that he will have a great game after 9...♕xd7? 10 ♕xb7, but gets a surprise: **9...0-0-0!**.

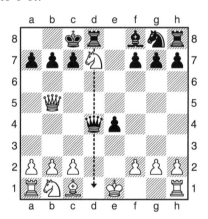

Now if the knight moves, Black will give instant mate on d1, while otherwise he recaptures the knight and keeps his extra pawn: **10 0-0 ♕xd7 11 ♕a5 a6 12 ♘c3 ♘f6 13 ♗g5 ♗e7** leaves White fighting for a draw in a very difficult position. Oddly, the same idea works if the pawn is back on e7 instead of e4, which can occur from a completely different opening: **1 e4 ♘f6 2 e5 ♘g8 3 d4 d6 4 ♘f3 ♗g4 5 ♗e2 dxe5 6 ♘xe5 ♗xe2 7 ♕xe2**

♕xd4 8 ♕b5+? ♘d7 9 ♘xd7 0-0-0! and Black is better. This version of the trap was recently used by a strong grandmaster.

Both sides made mistakes in our next example. **1 ♘f3 ♘f6 2 c4 c5 3 ♘c3 d5 4 cxd5 ♘xd5 5 e3 ♘xc3 6 bxc3 g6 7 ♗b5+ ♘d7 8 ♗a3 ♕c7 9 d4 cxd4? 10 ♕xd4!** (exploiting an *Uncompleted Fianchetto* – see Trap 72) **10...e5? 11 ♘xe5 ♗xa3 12 ♗xd7+??** (12 ♘g4! is very strong, as 12...0-0?? allows 13 ♘h6#) **12...♗xd7 13 ♘xd7**.

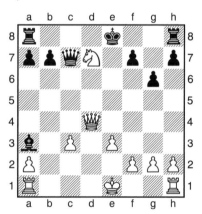

It looks like White is winning (for example, 13...♕xd7?? 14 ♕xh8+ or 13...♔e7?? 14 ♖d1), but a stunning move changes everything: **13...0-0-0!**. Black's rooks now protect each other and the once-proud knight is hopelessly pinned. After **14 0-0 ♕xd7 15 ♕xa7 ♗d6** Black went on to win in a game between two Hungarian masters.

TRAP 87 — Castle the Intruder: Kingside Edition

Making knights look silly for hundreds of years

Like the previous section, the idea is that in response to a knight landing next to the king on f2 (or f7), it may be effective simply to castle, and turn the tables on the knight that was so keen to attack.

The most famous example of this idea is a miniature game that you may have seen between Hoffman and Petrov from 1844. Rather than duplicate that complicated battle, I shall present some more clear-cut (and modern!) examples. **1 e4 e5 2 ♘f3 ♘c6 3 d4 exd4 4 ♗c4 ♗c5 5 c3 ♘f6 6 e5 d5 7 ♗b5 ♘e4 8 cxd4 ♗b4+ 9 ♘bd2 ♗g4?!** (it is simpler to castle and wait to see where this bishop should best be placed) **10 ♕a4! ♗xf3? 11 ♕xb4 ♕h4 12 gxf3! ♘xf2** (after 12...♕xf2+ 13 ♔d1 Black remains a piece down).

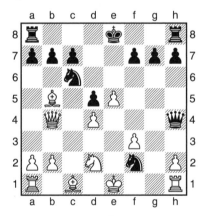

But now what? 13...♘d3++ is threatened. Must White lose his rook or queen? **13 0-0!!**. Suddenly it is clear that Black has nothing. **13...♘h3+ 14 ♔h1 h5** (14...♘f4 threatens ...♕h3, but 15 ♘b3 removes any danger) **15 ♕c3 ♖h6 16 ♘b3 ♖g6 17 ♗e3 f5 18 ♗d3** and in a game in France, Black chose to resign here.

Now let's see Black using this idea to turn the tables on White. It happens in the Max Lange Attack. **1 e4 e5 2 ♘f3 ♘c6 3 ♗c4 ♗c5 4 0-0 ♘f6 5 d4 exd4 6 e5 d5 7 exf6 dxc4 8 ♖e1+ ♗e6 9 ♘g5 ♕d5!** (in Trap 44 this centralizing move failed, but here it is good) **10 ♘c3 ♕f5 11 ♘ce4 ♗b6 12 ♘xf7?**.

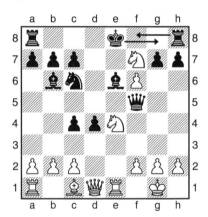

This dramatic move looks good at first (as 12...♗xf7?? loses the queen, and 12...♔xf7? 13 ♘g5+ ♔g8 14 fxg7! is complex but good for White), and a few dozen players have been tempted to try it. But after **12...0-0!!** White's knights must retreat in panic while the black forces use the open lines to attack with great force. Then **13 ♘fg5 ♗d5 14 fxg7 ♔xg7 15 f3 ♖ae8** gives Black a dominant position; one threat is the simple 16...h6. And after **13 ♘g3 ♕xf6 14 ♘g5 ♕xf2+ 15 ♔h1 ♗d5 16 ♖g1 d3 17 cxd3 ♕xg1+** Black soon won in a game played in Hungary.

TRAP 88   Winning the Queen at Too High a Cost

Don't guess: "Do the math"

A very common error at most levels of chess is overvaluing the queen. A player might sacrifice a piece or two to 'win' a queen for a rook or another piece, and only after doing a material count realize that he has actually lost material overall. The idea of 'winning the queen' is so ingrained in chess-players' minds that the normal logic when exchanging pieces goes out of the window.

1 d4 ♘f6 2 c4 e6 3 ♘f3 b6 4 g3 ♗b7 5 ♗g2 ♗e7 6 0-0 0-0 7 ♕c2 d5 8 ♘e5 c5 9 dxc5 ♗xc5 10 ♘c3 ♕c8 11 ♗g5 ♗e7?! (11...d4 is better) **12 cxd5! ♘xd5??**. Black thinks he is tricking his opponent, but it is the other way around. 12...exd5 is necessary, but leaves White with a good position – his pieces are excellently developed.

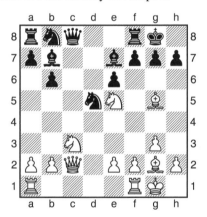

13 ♘xd5!. What's this? White is sacrificing his queen... but for a whole bucketload of pieces. **13...♕xc2 14 ♘xe7+ ♔h8 15 ♗xb7**. That's already three pieces, and the black rook is trapped in the corner on a8. **15...♕c7 16 ♘xf7+ ♖xf7 17 ♗xa8 ♘a6 18 ♖ac1**. Now Black mustn't allow ♖c8+, but after **18...♘c5 19 b4** he is losing yet another piece. This all happened in a game in the Bulgarian championship.

After **1 d4 ♘f6 2 ♘f3 c5 3 e3 g6 4 b3 ♗g7 5 ♗b2 cxd4 6 exd4 0-0 7 ♗d3 d5 8 0-0 ♘c6 9 ♖e1 ♘b4**, White could simply retreat his bishop by 10 ♗f1. After 10...♗f5 11 ♘a3 followed by c3 the position is perfectly normal and he has nothing to complain about. Instead with **10 ♗a3?** White embarks on a reckless adventure that ends in disaster because he didn't count the material carefully enough.

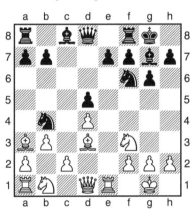

10...♘xd3 11 ♗xe7?? (11 cxd3 is better, even though it leaves White with a weak pawn-structure) **11...♘xe1 12 ♗xd8 ♘xf3+ 13 ♕xf3 ♖xd8**. The dust has settled. White has 'won' the black queen in exchange for a rook and two bishops. That's worth way more than a queen, and Black will win the game easily.

Count the Material *Before* Sacrificing

Like driving the car straight off the cliff

Overvaluing the queen is such a common error that it deserves a second section. In these two examples, players go out of their way to *force* a position where they have lost too much in return for the queen they have won. Remove the blinkers: add up the material before you take the plunge!

1 e4 c5 2 d4 cxd4 3 c3 dxc3 4 ♘xc3 e6 5 ♘f3 a6 6 ♗c4 b5 7 ♗b3 ♗b7 8 ♕e2 ♘c6 9 0-0 ♘ge7 10 ♖d1. This move misses the target. White hopes to make something of a pin on the d-file, but it doesn't work. Without going too far into opening theory, 10 ♗g5 causes Black more problems, planning to meet 10...h6 (10...f6 leaves the e6-pawn less well defended) 11 ♗e3 ♘g6?! with 12 ♘d5! (compare this with the sacrifices we see in Trap 93). **10...♘g6 11 ♘g5?! ♗c5 12 ♗xe6?? fxe6 13 ♘xe6**.

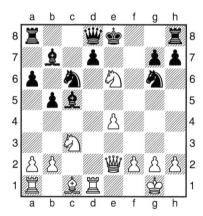

White must have assumed the black queen would now move, and was happy with the situation. Indeed, 13...♕e7?? 14 ♘d5 is good for White, but the queen does not have to move at all: **13...dxe6! 14 ♖xd8+ ♖xd8**. White is not just hopelessly down on material, but his kingside will come under attack; e.g., **15 ♗g5 ♖d7 16 ♕g4 0-0 17 ♕xe6+**

♖df7 18 ♗e3 ♘d4 19 ♕g4 ♘f4 and Black soon won in a game played in Germany.

After **1 e4 c5 2 c3 d5 3 exd5 ♕xd5 4 d4 ♘f6 5 ♘f3 ♘c6 6 dxc5 ♕xc5 7 ♘a3**, 7...e5 is a good option. **7...♘g4?!** is unwise, as it is based on a tactic that doesn't work. After **8 ♕e2 ♗f5 9 h3**, the error **9...♗d3?** is the most common move, but White can now give up his queen in return for a king's ransom! (9...♘ge5 is safer, but Black's knight manoeuvre has wasted time.)

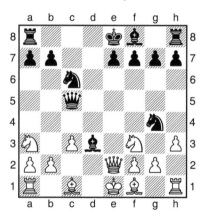

10 ♕xd3! is practically forced, but strong. **10...♕xf2+ 11 ♔d1 ♖d8**. This was the point: the white queen is pinned and lost. But after **12 ♕xd8+ ♔xd8 13 hxg4** White has rook, bishop and knight for queen and pawn – a significant material advantage – and excellent winning chances. He will slowly complete his development, while the black queen does not pose much of a threat on its own.

TRAP 90   Winning the Queen, Losing the King

It's the one piece you can never afford to trade

As we have seen, it's a common error to give up way too much material in order to win the enemy queen. A more classic trap is winning the queen at the cost of king safety. Here are some nice examples.

1 c4 c5 2 g3 ♘f6 3 ♗g2 d5 4 cxd5 ♘xd5 5 ♘c3 ♘c7 6 ♕a4+ ♗d7 7 ♕b3 ♘c6 8 ♕xb7. White's raid with his queen has won a pawn at the cost of some time. Black should now seek compensation with 8...♘d4, centralizing his knight and creating some threats. In a few games Black thought that he could win the white queen with **8...♖b8??**.

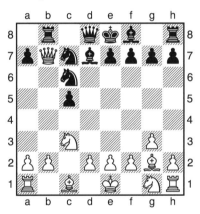

However, this misses the fact that Black's king is in danger. After **9 ♕xc6! ♗xc6 10 ♗xc6+** it's not mate, but the only way out of check is **10...♕d7 11 ♗xd7+**, which leaves Black a piece down with a hopeless game.

You should be careful when pinning pieces against the queen. Unlike a pin against the king, it is legal for the pinned piece to move. Take a look at the position after **1 e4 e5 2 ♘f3 ♘c6 3 d4 exd4 4 ♘xd4 ♗c5 5 ♘b3 ♗b6 6 a4 a6 7 ♘c3 ♘f6 8 ♗g5 h6 9 ♗h4 d6**. Now **10 ♘d5?** appears powerful,

ganging up on the pinned knight on f6. But after the queen sacrifice **10...♘xe4!!** it doesn't look quite so smart.

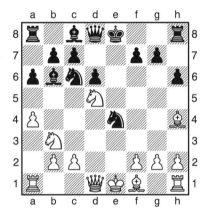

The main point is that **11 ♗xd8?** walks into **11...♗xf2+ 12 ♔e2 ♗g4+ 13 ♔d3 ♘e5+ 14 ♔xe4 f5+ 15 ♔f4 ♘g6#**, a beautiful mating sequence that has occurred in a couple of games. The start of this looks like Legall's Mate (Trap 66), but the end is different. Still, a player familiar with the Legall theme might have spotted the danger and looked for a way out. There is in fact a way for White to stay in the game: **11 ♕h5!**. After **11...g5 12 ♗c4** (or **12 ♗d3 ♘c5**) **12...♘e5 13 ♕e2 0-0 14 ♕xe4 gxh4** White is worse, but may yet survive in a complex struggle.

The moral is clear: if you are hit by a surprise move, don't panic! There might be a saving idea, but you'll need to give yourself a chance to find it.

Queen Check Met by b4 Shocker

The queen on a worse square. Cost: one pawn. Bargain!

It's a standard way to escape a sticky situation: throw in a queen check, gaining a free move. But the opponent blocks the check with a 'pointless' pawn move. OK, the pawn attacks the queen, but so what? The queen can take the pawn, again with check. But it becomes clear that the queen is now much less well placed. This is the b4 Shocker!

1 e4 c6 2 d4 d5 3 ♘c3 g6 4 ♘f3 ♗g4 5 h3 ♗xf3 6 ♕xf3 e6 7 h4 ♗g7 8 ♗e3 dxe4? 9 ♘xe4. Black has made too many pawn moves – the pawn on e6 is not helping his development. With **9...♘f6** he walks into a pin, thinking he has a way out. However, there is a cruel surprise coming his way! With **10 ♗g5 ♕a5+?** (10...♘bd7 11 ♘d6+ is unpleasant for Black, but he is not instantly losing) Black was no doubt dreaming of 11 ♗d2 ♕d8 12 ♗g5, repeating the position, but it is time for the Shocker: **11 b4!**.

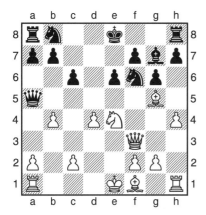

11...♕xb4+. Any other move loses the knight on f6. **12 c3 ♕b2**. Will the attack on the a1-rook save Black? **13 ♘xf6+ ♗xf6 14 ♕xf6**. No, because White threatens mate on e7. After **14...♕xc3+? 15 ♔e2 ♕c2+ 16 ♔e3** White wins because **16...♕c3+ 17 ♗d3** is the end of the checks and **17...0-0 18 ♗h6** is the end of Black's king. Instead

after **14...♕xa1+ 15 ♔e2** the checks eventually run out and White will mate or win a lot of material.

This type of idea can occur on many other squares, but in the opening it is most common for it to be a black queen check on a5 met by the pawn moving to b4. **1 e4 d5 2 exd5 ♕xd5 3 ♘c3 ♕a5 4 d4 ♘c6** (starting a fight in the centre) **5 ♗d2 ♘xd4 6 ♘b5 ♕b6 7 ♗e3 ♕a5+??** (instead of this greedy move, 7...e5 keeps Black afloat) **8 b4!**. This surprising move seems to throw in a pawn for nothing, but there is a sneaky purpose. **8...♕xb4+ 9 c3**.

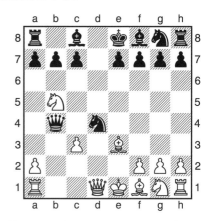

The queen is attacked and there is no time to save the knight on d4. Black loses a piece after **9...♕a5 10 ♕xd4!**, when **10...a6** (hoping to trap the b5-knight) **11 ♖d1! c6 12 ♕b6! 1-0** was the neat and instructive finish of an old game in the British championship.

The potential threat can become real in the blink of an eye

Sudden tactics on the h-file can appear out of nowhere and dramatically change the course of the game. A rook rampaging on the h-file is a threat to the enemy king whether it is castled or not.

In our first example, a mate threat turns things around. **1 e4 ♘f6 2 e5 ♘d5 3 d4 d6 4 ♘f3 ♗g4 5 ♗e2 c6 6 0-0 ♗xf3 7 ♗xf3 dxe5 8 dxe5 e6 9 ♕e2 ♘d7 10 c4 ♘e7 11 b3 ♘g6 12 ♗b2 ♕c7**. This is a tricky position for White, as his e5-pawn is vulnerable. He finds a way to sacrifice it, but it fails for a subtle reason. **13 ♗h5?! ♘dxe5! 14 f4 ♘d7 15 f5**.

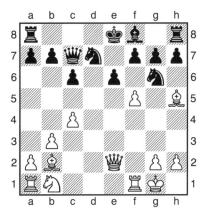

"White has activated his pieces and is ripping into Black's game, exploiting the king caught in the centre." Did you believe that? None of it is true: White has been caught in a known opening trap. **15...0-0-0!!** turns the story on its head! **16 fxg6?! hxg6!** opens the h-file with the point that if the bishop moves, White is mated on h2. **16 fxe6 fxe6** isn't much of an improvement as Black's pieces are flooding out and have plenty of targets to attack. I had the black side of this in a key game in an English counties championship final. As this helped my team become

national champions, I basically won a nice trophy for knowing one opening trap!

Next up: an h-file pin lets a bishop take up residence close to the enemy king. **1 d4 ♘f6 2 ♗g5 ♘e4 3 h4 c6 4 ♘d2 ♘xg5 5 hxg5**. An unusual opening has given White an open h-file. But how can he use it? In a grandmaster game, Black felt that he couldn't, and that it was safe to go pawn-grabbing: **5...♕b6?! 6 e3 ♕xb2?! 7 g6!**. The pin on the h-file means Black must take with the f-pawn, leaving his king exposed. **7...fxg6 8 ♗d3 d5 9 ♗xg6+**.

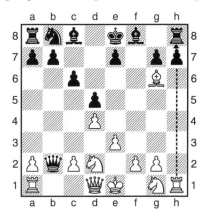

The bishop is untouchable thanks to the pin. After **9...♔d8 10 ♘gf3** White has a huge advantage, and the game (between Kosić and Marković) was very one-sided from here on: **10...♗g4 11 ♖b1 ♕c3 12 ♖xb7 ♘d7 13 ♕b1 ♗xf3 14 gxf3 e5 15 ♖xd7+ ♔xd7 16 ♕b7+ ♔e6 17 ♖h5**. The rook itself now comes into the attack via the h-file. **17...hxg6 18 ♖xe5+ ♔f6 19 ♕d7 1-0**.

Standard ♘d5 Sacrifice

Unleash a firestorm on the c-file

Some sacrifices arise naturally in certain structures. One example is a ♘d5 sacrifice to open the c-file, creating a pin against a black queen that has been unwisely placed on c7.

We turn to the Morra Gambit for a clear-cut example. **1 e4 c5 2 d4 cxd4 3 c3 dxc3 4 ♘xc3 ♘c6 5 ♗c4 e6 6 ♘f3 d6 7 ♕e2 a6 8 0-0 ♕c7**. With the c-file open, the queen is exposed here. In a typical Sicilian, White would have a pawn on c2 and the queen would be safer. **9 ♖d1 b5?!**. Another risky move. Now the c6-knight is less well defended. We shall soon see why this matters. **10 ♗b3 ♗e7 11 ♗f4 ♘f6?!** (11...♘e5 is a better try) **12 ♖ac1 0-0**. Black is unaware of the danger. **13 ♘d5!**. Here is the thematic sacrifice, though we can see immediately that it is no sacrifice at all, as White regains the piece right away.

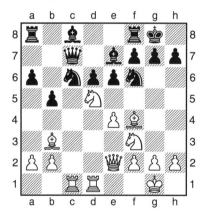

13...exd5 14 exd5 ♗g4 (14...♗b7? 15 dxc6 ♗xc6 16 ♘d4 costs Black a piece more on the c-file) **15 dxc6**. White has a huge advantage. His c6-pawn is strong, all his pieces are well-placed, and the d6-pawn is weak.

Now let's see another typical situation: White *does* have a c-pawn, but it is on c4,

ready to recapture on d5 after the knight sacrifice. **1 e4 c5 2 ♘f3 d6 3 d4 cxd4 4 ♘xd4 ♘f6 5 f3 a6 6 c4 e6 7 ♘c3 ♗e7 8 ♗e3 0-0 9 ♗e2 ♕c7 10 0-0 b6 11 ♖c1 ♗b7 12 ♕e1 ♘c6??** (12...♘bd7 avoids the deadly c-file pin; then a tough fight lies ahead).

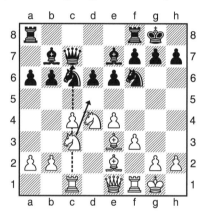

This pawn-structure is known as the hedgehog. Black's *pawns* on a6, b6, d6 and e6 are designed to work like spikes, keeping White's pieces at bay. But for this plan to work, Black's *pieces* need to be better placed. The way they are lined up on the c-file gives White a way to blast his way in. **13 ♘d5! ♕d8**. Black declines, but White now has a choice of strong options, as you would expect after lobbing a grenade into the heart of Black's position. 13...exd5 14 cxd5 followed by taking on c6 leaves Black a pawn down with a miserable game. **14 ♘xc6 ♗xc6 15 ♗xb6 ♕d7 16 ♘xe7+ ♕xe7 17 ♗d4** and White has won a pawn for nothing.

Amazing Intermezzos

All-out tactical warfare

An intermezzo is a move that suddenly breaks an expected sequence of moves, such as captures, and takes the game in a dramatically different path. We are about to see two incredible examples. Take your time to understand what is going on in them.

1 e4 c5 2 ♘f3 g6 3 c4 ♗g7 4 d4 ♕a5+ 5 ♘c3 ♘c6 6 ♗e3?! ♘f6 is a treacherous position for White, who is under attack on the central squares. **7 ♕d2?** is the obvious move, but lets Black demonstrate his idea: **7...cxd4 8 ♘xd4 ♘xe4!!**. Setting the board on fire! This move looks like pure black magic, but the logic is clear: Black uncovers an attack on d4. Now 9 ♘xe4 ♕xd2+ removes a defender of the d4-knight, so Black regains his piece after 10 ♔xd2 ♘xd4, keeping an extra pawn. With **9 ♘xc6**, planning to play ♘xe4 next move, White perhaps believes he has tricked Black.

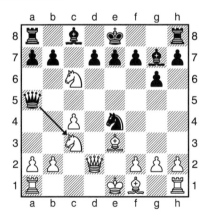

Both queens are attacked, and the position is very confusing. **9...♕xc3!!**. Black answers an intermezzo with an intermezzo! It is a hard move to spot because it looks like Black is giving his queen away, but it was attacked anyway, and White can't save his own queen. After **10 bxc3 ♘xd2 11 ♔xd2 dxc6**

Black is a pawn up with a great position. This is the end of the combination, but let's continue two moves to see another of our traps in action: **12 ♖b1? ♗f5 13 ♖xb7? 0-0-0+!** (see Trap 27).

1 e4 c5 2 ♘f3 ♘c6 3 d4 cxd4 4 ♘xd4 g6 5 ♘c3 ♗g7 6 ♗e3 ♘f6 7 ♗c4 ♕a5 8 0-0 ♕b4?!. The idea behind this move doesn't work. **9 ♗b3 ♘xe4?**. It is remarkable how often this blunder has been played, *and how often White has failed to punish it*. **10 ♘xc6!!**. This simple-looking move is based on a clever idea. (10 ♘xe4? ♘xd4 was Black's basic point.) **10...dxc6** (10...bxc6 11 a3! ♘xc3 12 ♕f3! is similar) **11 a3!**.

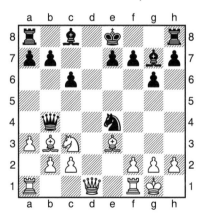

11...♘xc3 (a queen move loses the knight on e4) **12 ♕f3!**. Here we see the problem: Black can't save his queen without allowing a disaster on f7. After **12...♘e2+ 13 ♔h1!** Black must give up his queen by **13...♕xb3**, but this is hopeless in the long run.

TRAP 95 — ♘xe5 and ♕h5+: Success and Failure

Judge each case strictly on its merits

A knight sacrifice for a pawn on e5 followed by a queen check on h5 can be a devastating way to bring the queen into the attack. In other cases it may be a useful exchanging manoeuvre. And sometimes it fails completely! With any tactical operation, the opponent's ideas must be taken into account before we dive in. Here we look at two extreme cases, both played at master level.

1 e4 e5 2 ♗c4 ♘f6 3 d3 d5 4 exd5 ♘xd5 5 ♘f3 ♘c6 6 0-0 ♗e7 7 ♖e1 f6 8 h3 ♘b6 9 ♗b3 ♘a5??. Black wants to remove the b3-bishop. This is understandable as this piece is staring into the heart of Black's kingside, but this move takes Black's eye off the centre.

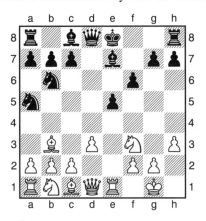

10 ♘xe5! fxe5 (there is no time to play 10...♘xb3 due to 11 ♕h5+ g6 12 ♘xg6) **11 ♕h5+ ♔d7** (11...g6 12 ♕xe5 attacks the pieces on a5 and h8) **12 ♕xe5 ♘xb3 13 ♗g5!.** Now Black can't save his e7-bishop without allowing mate: 13...♖e8 14 ♕e6#. 13...♗xg5 14 ♕e6# is again mate, while **13...♘xa1 14 ♗xe7 ♕g8 15 ♕b5+!** is a longer forced mate: **15...c6 16 ♕f5+ ♔c7** (16...♔e8 17 ♗g5+) **17 ♗d6+ ♔xd6 18 ♕e5+ ♔d7 19 ♕e7#.**

So that time the sacrifice was successful. Now it is time for the opposite extreme,

where the idea fails due to a countertactic. As Black is making the sacrifice this time, it is on e4 and the queen check is on h4. **1 d4 ♘f6 2 c4 g6 3 ♘c3 ♗g7 4 e4 d6 5 ♗e2 0-0 6 ♗g5 ♘a6 7 ♕d2 e5 8 d5 ♗d7?!.** This looks like an ordinary move, but it has unfortunate consequences. After **9 f3!?** Black's normal freeing idea will fail for a very subtle reason. But Black plays it anyhow: **9...h6?? 10 ♗xh6! ♘xe4 11 ♘xe4 ♕h4+ 12 g3 ♕xh6.**

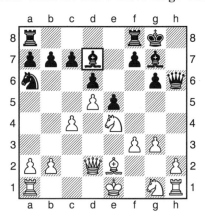

This is a standard exchanging manoeuvre by Black in the King's Indian Defence. But there is snag here: **13 ♘f6+!.** If the bishop were on c8 rather than d7, Black could put his king on h8 and have an excellent game. But here the knight attacks his bishop and he is losing a piece. 13...♗xf6 drops the queen, while 13...♔h8 14 ♕xh6+ ♗xh6 15 ♘xd7 ♖fd8 16 ♘f6 is obviously hopeless for Black.

TRAP 96 — Sizzling Long-Diagonal Skewer

Don't just count attackers and defenders

Each central square is on a long diagonal, and at the end of that diagonal is a rook – at least until it is developed. This basic piece of geometry can allow us to pick off a pawn thanks to a skewer that comes at the end of a big sequence of exchanges. It's an idea that is often overlooked but can be tremendously effective.

1 ♘f3 ♘f6 2 d4 g6 3 ♗f4 ♗g7 4 e3 d6 5 h3 0-0 6 ♗e2 ♘bd7 7 0-0 e6 8 c4 ♕e7 9 ♘c3 e5 10 ♗h2 e4?! 11 ♘d2. The e4-pawn is attacked twice and defended twice, which would usually mean it is safe. With **11...b6?** Black continues to develop and intends ...♗b7, supporting his e4-pawn once more.

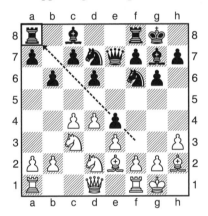

But the move is a blunder. This position has arisen several times, with strong players as White. But amazingly, in only one of those games has White played **12 ♘cxe4!**, winning a pawn due to a skewer on the long diagonal: **12...♘xe4 13 ♘xe4 ♕xe4** (13...♗b7 14 ♘c3 leaves White a good pawn up) **14 ♗f3**, followed by ♗xa8.

In the next example, the sequence of exchanges before the skewer is even longer, but the basic concept is the same. **1 e4 ♘f6 2 e5 ♘d5 3 d4 d6 4 ♘f3 ♗g4 5 ♗e2 c6 6 0-0 ♗xf3 7 ♗xf3 dxe5 8 dxe5 e6 9 ♖e1 ♘d7 10**

c4 ♘e7 11 ♗d2 ♕c7 12 ♗c3 ♘g6 13 ♕e2. Attacked three times and defended three times... For the moment the e5-pawn is safe, but that can easily change. **13...♖d8.** This move prevents the obvious 14 ♘d2? because 14...♘dxe5! 15 ♗xe5 ♕xe5 16 ♕xe5 ♘xe5 17 ♖xe5 ♖xd2 picks off the loose knight on d2. **14 b4?!.** White stops ...♘c5, which has ideas of both ...♘d3 and ...♘a4. However, this is no big deal, and 14 g3 is preferable. **14...♗e7** creates a hidden threat.

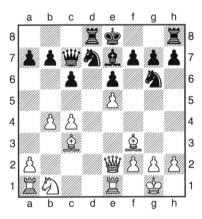

15 g3?. It's hard to believe, but this allows a long-diagonal skewer. (15 ♕b2 avoids disaster because 15...♘dxe5? loses to 16 ♖xe5! ♘xe5 17 ♗xe5.) **15...♘dxe5!** and Black wins a pawn due to **16 ♗xe5 ♕xe5 17 ♕xe5 ♘xe5 18 ♖xe5 ♗f6**, skewering the rooks on e5 and a1. This trick once helped me achieve a quick and easy win against an international master.

Traps in the Chigorin

Playing with fire

The Chigorin Defence to the Queen's Gambit, 1 d4 d5 2 c4 ♘c6, leads to play unlike any other opening, with traps for both sides. These two end well for White.

1 d4 d5 2 c4 ♘c6 3 ♘c3 ♘f6 4 ♘f3 ♗g4?! 5 cxd5 ♘xd5 6 e4 ♘xc3 7 bxc3 e5 8 d5 ♘b8 9 ♕a4+ ♘d7 10 ♘xe5 ♕f6.

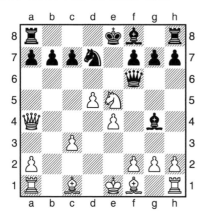

In the mid-1980s, this was a topical position, where Black's resources were yet to be tamed. Take a while to try to work out what is going on, and why certain strong-looking moves might not work. White's best path is very subtle, and I had the privilege to see it being played 'live' for the first time at a tournament in Switzerland. **11 ♗e2!!**. What? Just this little bishop move? It turns out that Black's bishop is overloaded, and this nudge is all it takes to bring Black's position crashing down. Now 11...♗xe2? 12 ♕xd7# is instant mate, while 11...c6 12 dxc6 ♕xe5 13 cxd7+ ♗xd7 14 ♕d4 leaves White a pawn up for nothing. **11...♕xe5 12 ♗xg4 ♕xc3+? 13 ♗d2 ♕xa1+ 14 ♔e2** is one of those wonderful 'take my rooks!' moments, as **14...♕xh1** allows **15 ♕xd7#.**

1 d4 d5 2 c4 ♘c6 3 ♘c3 dxc4 4 ♘f3 ♗g4?! 5 d5! ♗xf3 (5...♘a5 6 ♕a4+ c6 7 b4! is bad for Black) and now **6 exf3!** is the right recapture. White's development advantage outweighs all other factors. **6...♘e5 7 ♗f4 ♘g6** (7...♘d3+ 8 ♗xd3 cxd3 offers White a choice of strong moves, including 9 ♕b3).

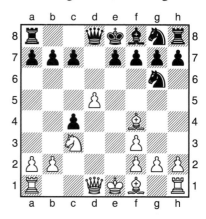

If White retreats his bishop, Black will be able to develop his kingside. But there is something better: **8 ♗xc4!**. Earlier in the book we saw tricks based on a deadly ♗b5+, so this idea should not come as too great a surprise. **8...♘xf4? 9 ♗b5+ c6 10 dxc6** is a clear win for White, but otherwise Black has no good options. After **8...♘f6 9 ♗g3** Black isn't just behind in development, but he has no way to catch up. With the bishop on c4, Black can only advance his e-pawn as a giveaway. White will finish his development and then start a very one-sided fight. I had this pleasure in a Cambridge-Oxford match once.

TRAP 98   The Case for the Defence

The devil is in the detail

We have seen many games where the attacker won. But in practice the defender often comes out on top, and there are nice ideas to be found when facing an attack too. Not every sacrifice is correct, but we must often dig deep to see why.

1 e4 e6 2 d4 d5 3 ♘d2 dxe4 4 ♘xe4 ♗e7 5 ♘f3 ♘d7 6 ♘fg5 ♘gf6 7 ♘xf7?. This looks similar to some successful sacrifices that we have seen, so what is different this time? White doesn't have reinforcements *immediately* ready, and his own king is exposed. How should Black make use of these factors? After **7...♔xf7 8 ♘g5+ ♔g8! 9 ♘xe6**, Black's next move is critical.

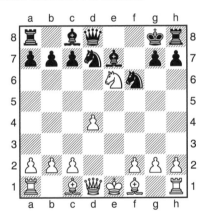

A German championship game featured 9...♕e8?. White then played 10 ♘xc7??, allowing the sensational snap mate 10...♗b4#!. However, 10 ♗c4! gives White a devastating attack, as he has now brought in enough reinforcements and can answer 10...♗b4+ with 11 ♔f1. Black should play **9...♗b4+! 10 c3 ♕e7**. The queen uses the square gifted to it by the bishop, and Black is now comfortably on top. **11 ♕e2** (not 11 ♗c4 ♘b6 followed by ...♗xe6) **11...♘b6 12 ♘g5 ♗d6 13 ♕xe7 ♗xe7 14 ♗d3 ♗d7** and Black, with a piece

for two pawns, went on to win. This was also a game in Germany, though well below championship level. Ordinary players sometimes show the grandmasters how it's done!

1 d4 ♘f6 2 c4 e6 3 ♘c3 ♗b4 4 ♕c2 0-0 5 e3 b6 6 ♗d3 c5 7 ♘e2 cxd4 8 exd4 d5 9 0-0?! (White should exchange on d5, since his pieces are better set up for the structure that arises after 9 cxd5 exd5) **9...dxc4 10 ♗xh7+??**. Spotting a tactic, but it fails. He has nothing better than 10 ♗xc4, though this is not a good IQP position for White, as his pieces are not very active. **10...♘xh7 11 ♕e4**.

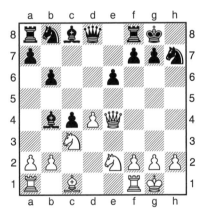

The rook is trapped in the corner, but after **11...♕d7!**, White realized that his queen would not escape that same corner following 12 ♕xa8 ♘c6 and ...♗b7. This game was from a qualifying event for the postal world championship – but long before the days when computers became relevant!

111

TRAP 99 — The Most Basic Blunder of Them All

If in doubt, play it out

If you think your position is hopeless, make sure you have exhausted all your chances before throwing in the towel. Here we look at two games where players resigned in positions that would have been OK for them, if only they had been able to find the saving resource.

1 e4 c5 2 ♘f3 e6 3 d4 cxd4 4 ♘xd4 ♘c6 5 ♘c3 a6 6 ♗e3 ♗b4 7 ♗d3 ♘ge7 8 f4 d5 9 e5?! ♘xd4 10 ♗xd4 ♘c6 11 ♗e2 ♕a5 12 0-0 ♘xd4 13 ♕xd4. Now a simple move like 13...♗d7 gives Black an excellent position. However, in one game he saw what looked like a chance to win on the spot, and went for it: **13...♗c5?!**.

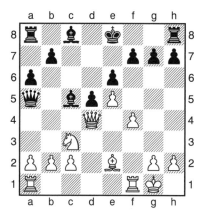

White resigned as his queen is pinned against his king. But he had an escape clause here: **14 ♗b5+!** leaves White no worse after 14...♗d7 15 ♕xc5 axb5 (and certainly not 15...♗xb5?? 16 a4), while 14...♕xb5?! 15 ♘xb5 ♗xd4+ 16 ♘xd4 is an unpleasant endgame for Black, as his bishop is 'bad'.

1 e4 e5 2 ♘f3 ♘c6 3 ♗b5 a6 4 ♗a4 ♘f6 5 d4 ♘xe4 6 d5 ♘e7 (6...♘c5 is a good alternative) **7 ♘xe5 b5?! 8 ♗b3 ♗b7?!** (8...d6 is preferable) **9 d6?!** (9 ♕e2 is a better way to keep Black under pressure)

9...♘xd6 10 ♕xd6 was played in a game where Capablanca had White. His opponent, Meyer, chose to resign at this point, seeing that he was about to be mated on f7.

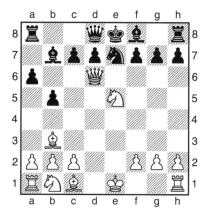

However, there is the remarkable saving move **10...♘d5!!**, when White can't simply keep his extra piece because his queen is trapped. 11 ♕xd7+ ♕xd7 12 ♘xd7 ♔xd7 13 0-0 leads to a more or less level endgame, and 11 ♕xd5 ♗xd5 12 ♗xd5 ♕f6 is highly unclear as 13 ♗xa8? ♕xe5+ 14 ♔d1 ♕d4+ followed by ...c6 traps the white bishop.

So don't rush to resign. A 'brilliant' resignation will impress no one. Always look for that last resource, however sure you might be that none exists. If you have a completely forced move, play it and get to the position that you think is hopeless. When it appears on the board, you might notice that there is actually a saving idea.

Playing an ordinary move is OK too

Sometimes players try too hard to make something dramatic happen. If there isn't anything dramatic to do, this can lead to disaster. Here are a couple of examples where 'playing for the maximum' leads straight to a loss.

1 d4 ♘f6 2 ♘c3 c5 3 ♗g5 cxd4 4 ♕xd4 ♘c6 5 ♕h4 ♕a5 6 0-0-0 d6 7 e4 ♗e6 8 a3 h6. An unusual opening has led to a normal-looking position where White could play either 9 ♗d2 or 9 ♗xf6 with reasonable chances. In one game White wanted more, but only ended up tricking himself: **9 f4??**

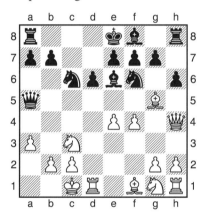

White takes advantage of the pin on the h-file to keep Black guessing a move or two longer. However, he has missed something important: **9...♘h7!**. Suddenly the pin is broken and the bishop is trapped. Knights don't typically go to squares like this, but we mustn't be blind to these moves. After **10 ♘f3 f6** White had seen enough and resigned.

We end with a grandmaster game from 2018. **1 d4 ♘f6 2 ♗g5 d5 3 e3 c6 4 ♗d3 ♗g4 5 ♘e2 ♘bd7 6 f3 ♗h5 7 0-0 ♗g6 8 c4 e6 9 cxd5 ♗xd3**. So far the play has been relatively normal. But with his next move,

White clearly assumed that his opponent had made a simple oversight. It pays to check very carefully in such cases that the oversight is not in fact ours.

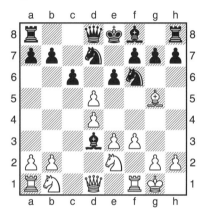

10 dxc6??. This type of intermezzo often wins a pawn if Black is forced to recapture (i.e. 10...bxc6?? 11 ♕xd3 leaves White a pawn up). But here he isn't! White should just play the simple 10 ♕xd3, when he has chances of pushing forward in the centre with the e4 advance and enjoying a normal opening advantage. 10 dxe6?? fails in the same way: 10...♗xe2! 11 exd7+ ♘xd7!!. **10...♗xe2!** and White resigned in Sengupta-Narayanan, Kolkata 2018. A move too late, White saw the problem: **11 cxd7+ ♘xd7!!** (11...♕xd7?? 12 ♕xe2 gives White an extra pawn) wins a piece for Black since both queens are attacked: 12 ♕xe2 ♕xg5 or 12 ♗xd8 ♗xd1 13 ♖xd1 ♖xd8.

Test Your Opening Tactics

In each of the following 48 diagrams, your task is to find the winning move for White or Black. You are not necessarily looking for a forced checkmate – just a clear way to get a very big advantage. In one case you need to answer a question.

If you have read the book carefully, you should be able to work out many of the answers. Even though these exact positions have not occurred in the book so far, most of the ideas have been mentioned, and very similar tactical traps have been highlighted. But remember that even when you have seen an almost identical position before, you can't assume that the same tactic works. You need to take into account any new defensive ideas.

If you are really stuck, then I have given a hint by telling you which Trap idea the exercise is based on. The exercises start off easy, and get much harder.

Target Scores
Give yourself 1 point for each winning move found. If you answered correctly only after looking at the hint, then you get ½ point.

42-48	**Master or grandmaster standard**
35-41	**Excellent club level**
28-34	**Very good opening skills**
21-27	**You are a dangerous opening tactician**
14-20	**Join a chess club!**
7-13	**Good, but read the book again**
0-6	**You were meant to steal the cheese, not cut it!**

THE WEAKEST SQUARE

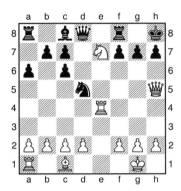

1) White wins
Hint: See Trap 54

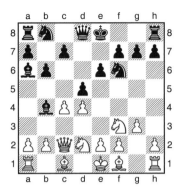

2) White wins
Hint: See Traps 31 and 73

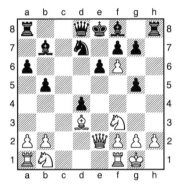

3) White wins
Hint: See Trap 4

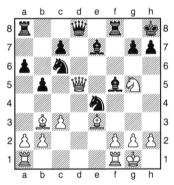

4) White wins
Hint: See Trap 67

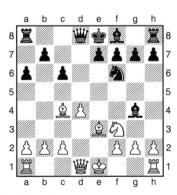

5) White wins
Hint: See Trap 11

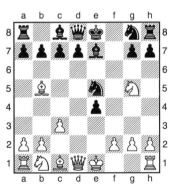

6) White wins
Hint: See Trap 17

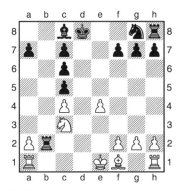

7) White wins
Hint: See Trap 27

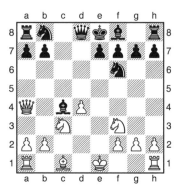

8) Black wins
Hint: See Trap 30

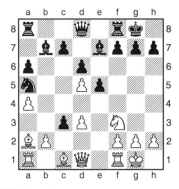

9) White wins
Hint: See Trap 41

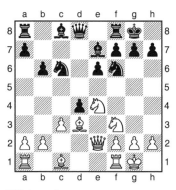

10) White wins
Hint: See Trap 7

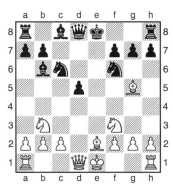

11) Black wins
Hint: See Trap 12

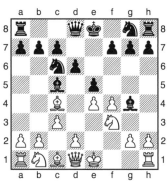

12) Should White play ♗xf7+ here?
Hint: See Trap 13

116

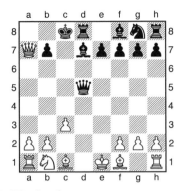

13) Black wins
Hint: See Trap 68

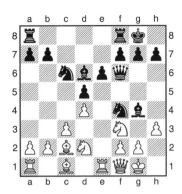

14) Black wins
Hint: See Trap 6

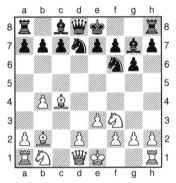

15) White wins
Hint: See Trap 16

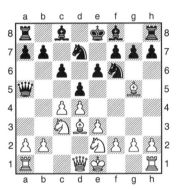

16) Black wins
Hint: See Trap 28

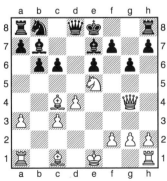

17) White wins
Hint: See Trap 50

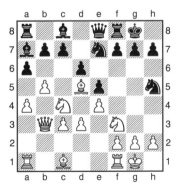

18) Black wins
Hint: See Trap 40

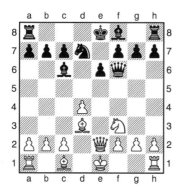

19) White wins
Hint: See Trap 45

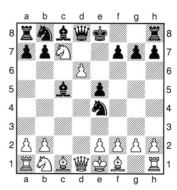

20) Black wins
Hint: See Trap 90

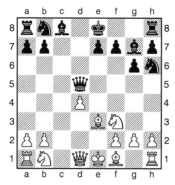

21) White wins
Hint: See Trap 25

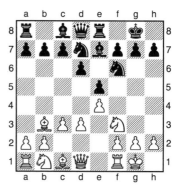

22) White wins
Hint: See Trap 48

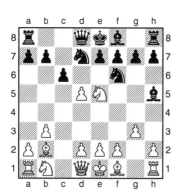

23) Black wins
Hint: See Trap 72

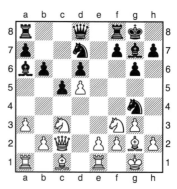

24) White wins
Hint: See Trap 32

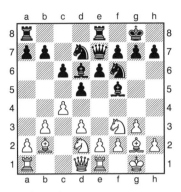

25) White wins
Hint: See Trap 19

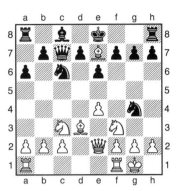

26) Black wins
Hint: See Trap 24

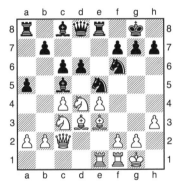

27) Black wins
Hint: See Trap 29

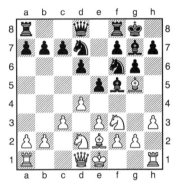

28) White wins
Hint: See Trap 41

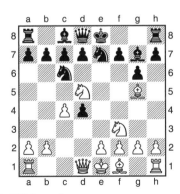

29) White wins
Hint: See Trap 3

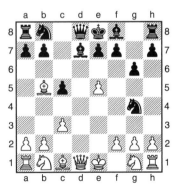

30) White wins
Hint: See Trap 58

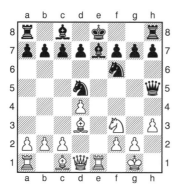

31) White wins
Hint: See Trap 78

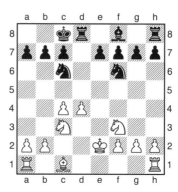

32) White wins
Hint: See Trap 51

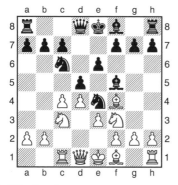

33) Black wins
Hint: See Trap 80

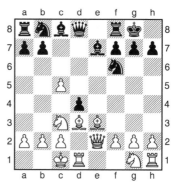

34) Black wins
Hint: See Trap 88

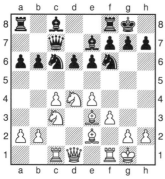

35) White wins
Hint: See Trap 93

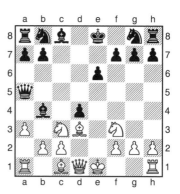

36) White wins
Hint: See Trap 43

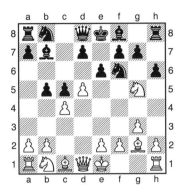

37) White wins
Hint: See Trap 39

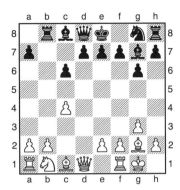

38) Black wins
Hint: See Trap 47

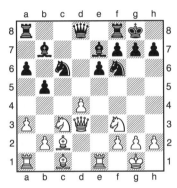

39) White wins
Hint: See Trap 83

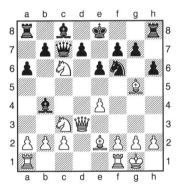

40) Black wins
Hint: See Trap 92

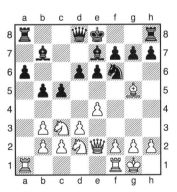

41) White wins
Hint: See Trap 33

42) Black wins
Hint: See Trap 36

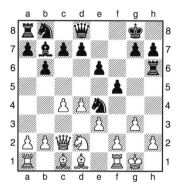

43) Black wins
Hint: See Trap 63

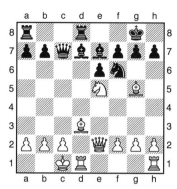

44) White wins
Hint: See Trap 64

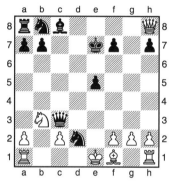

45) White wins
Hint: See Trap 86

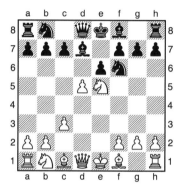

46) White wins
Hint: See Traps 39 and 77

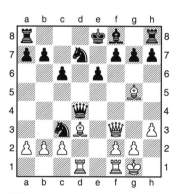

47) White wins
Hint: See Trap 74

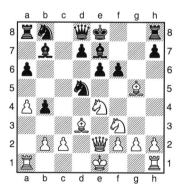

48) White wins
Hint: See Trap 84

Test Solutions

1. 14 ♕xh7+! ♔xh7 15 ♖h4# is the beautiful *Anastasia's Mate*.

2. 7 ♕a4+! wins a piece. You could view this as an example of either the *Overshot Bishop* or the *Exposed Bishop*. It's surprising that a world-class grandmaster allowed this simple tactic, and his opponent (a master) missed it. Perhaps the fact that the queen had already moved to c2 made it harder to spot.

3. It is like the *Snap Mate with Two Bishops*, but a pawn plays the role of one of the bishops: **14 ♕xe6+! fxe6** (interposing on e7 leaves Black a piece down) **15 ♗g6#**.

4. White mates by **16 ♕g8+! ♖xg8 17 ♘f7#** – a *Spectacular Smothered Mate*. Instead 16 ♘xe4? gives White just an extra pawn – a wasted opportunity. 16 ♘f7+?? seeks a 'Philidor's Legacy' smothered mate by 16...♔g8?? 17 ♘h6++ ♔h8 18 ♕g8+ ♖xg8 19 ♘f7# but 16...♖xf7 leaves Black better.

5. With **9 ♗xf7+! ♔xf7 10 ♘e5+ ♔g8 11 ♘xg4 ♘xg4 12 ♕xg4** White wins a pawn and destroys Black's position – his pawns are terrible and his king is horribly exposed. What is most surprising about this example is that it was a grandmaster who allowed it.

6. 8 ♘e6! makes use of the pinned d7-pawn to trap the black queen.

7. 11 0-0-0+! wins a rook by *Castling Queenside with Check*.

8. Black doesn't have to let White win back the bishop! As we saw in Trap 30, *A Bishop on e6* often *Provokes a Blunder*. After **8...b5!**

9 ♘xb5 ♗xb5 10 ♕xb5+ ♕d7 Black is a piece to the good.

9. Black has just innocently exchanged pawns on c3, assuming White will recapture. But White plays **14 b4!**, *Trapping the Knight*. This occurred in a game between masters. How could such a strong player miss this? Consider the position before Black played ...b4xc3. The b4-square is occupied, so it takes some imagination to spot that White can play b4 next move.

10. After **11 ♘xf6+! ♗xf6 12 ♕e4!** the *Double Attack with the Queen* against h7 (mate!) and the c6-knight wins a piece.

11. It's a *Disaster on f2*. **9...♗xf2+! 10 ♔xf2 ♘e4+** and after ...♘xg5 Black is a safe pawn up and has ruined White's kingside defences.

12. No, **6 ♗xf7+??** is a *Failed Discovery Trick* due to **6...♔xf7 7 ♘g5+ ♕xg5!**, when Black wins a piece; e.g., **8 ♕b3+ ♗e6 9 ♕xb7 ♕xg2!** and White can resign.

13. *Decoy and Double Check* force mate: **10...♕d1+!! 11 ♔xd1 ♗g4++ 12 ♔c2** (or 12 ♔e1 ♖d1#) **12...♗d1#**.

14. It's a *Junior Chess Special*: **13...♘xh3+!** deflects the white g-pawn so it no longer defends the f3-knight. After **14 gxh3 ♗xf3 15 ♘xf3 ♕xf3** Black was a strong pawn up and soon won in a game played in the Argentine (non-junior!) championship.

15. Here White's set-up is completely different from what we saw in Trap 16, but the same idea works: **7 ♗xf7+! ♔xf7 8 ♘g5+ ♔e8** (8...♔g8 9 ♕b3+ mates) **9 ♘e6** and the queen is trapped.

16. Putting the knight on e2 in the *Cambridge Springs* looks tempting as it defends its colleague on c3. But by failing to support the g5-bishop, it allows instant disaster after **7...dxc4!**. White isn't saved by **8 ♗xf6** because **8...cxd3!** attacks the knight that has just unwisely moved to e2.

17. The brutal sacrifice **13 ♘xf7!** *Drags the King Out*. **13...♔xf7 14 ♕xe6+ ♔e8 15 ♕f7+ ♔d7 16 ♗e6+ ♔c7 17 ♗f4+** forces mate (and the win of several black pieces along the way!). This was a game of mine about which I had mixed feelings. My opponent was a tireless organizer of local events in my town, and this wasn't a very polite way to thank him for his efforts!

18. White has impaled himself on Black's spikes. After **13...axb5 14 axb5** (14 ♕xb5 ♕xb5 15 axb5 ♗xf2+! is similar) White threatens to bury the bishop by playing b6, but it comes too late, as the *Dastardly a-File Discovery* **14...♗xf2+!** wins the rook on a1.

19. Yes, it's the *Grandmaster's Queen Trap*! But there is a little difference from the examples we saw in Trap 45: after **9 ♗g5! ♗xf3** it is no good to put the queen on d2 since after 10 ♕d2?? ♕xd4 there is no ♗b5+ discovered attack with check. But the fix is simple enough – the white queen has a square where it defends the d4-pawn directly: **10 ♕e3!** and the black queen is trapped.

20. In playing his last move, White must have not imagined that Black could give up his queen at all, since it is easy to calculate that Black wins by **8...♕xc7!**. The main point is the mate after 9 dxc7 ♗xf2#, while 9 ♕a4+ is met by 9...♕c6, snuffing out White's hope of regaining a knight on e4.

21. 8 ♕c1! wins a piece thanks to an *Invisible Double Attack* on c8 and h6. At least, it must be invisible, judging from the number of strong players who have allowed this move, and the number who have missed it – believe it or not, 8 ♘c3?? is actually the most common move.

22. Black has *Carelessly Allowed the ♗xf7+ Sacrifice*: **8 ♗xf7+! ♔xf7 9 ♘g5+** and ♘e6 wins the black queen.

23. With **7...♘xe5!** Black spots that the *Uncompleted Fianchetto* allows a fork by the queen. After **8 ♗xe5 ♕d5! 9 ♗xf6 ♕xh1** Black has made a decisive material gain.

24. The *Queen Fork* **13 ♕a4!** wins a piece. Black's last move, ...♘b8-d7??, was a terrible oversight. It left the bishop undefended on a6 *and* prevented it from defending the g4-knight by coming back to c8. It looked like a normal developing move in a position where White had no threats, but as we know, that does not mean a move is safe.

25. 11 e4!, followed by e5, is an example of how *Pawns Can Win Pieces!* We saw a very similar position in Trap 19.

26. I hope you weren't distracted by that white bishop on e7 and noticed the contours of the *Siberian Trap*. After **11...♘d4!** White loses his queen or is mated: 12 ♗a3 ♘xf3+ or 12 ♘xd4 ♕xh2#.

27. With **14...♗xh3!** Black *Sets Up a Knight Fork*. After **15 gxh3 ♗xd4 16 ♗xd4 ♘f3+** Black has won a pawn and shattered White's kingside defences. This was played in a very high-level game – in a Candidates tournament – so White resigned rather than watch as his opponent slowly converted his huge advantage into victory.

28. Here we have a *Bishop Trapped by Pawns*. Black's last move, ...e7-e5??, *self-pinned* the knight on f6. This allows White to play **9 e4!** and because the knight on d7 blocks the bishop's retreat, it only has the move **9...♗e6** but then **10 d5** completes the trapping of the bishop.

29. **7 ♘xd4!** gives White a big advantage thanks to the *Mating-Net with Bishop and Knight*: **7...♗xd4** (7...♘xd4 8 ♗xe7 and 7...0-0 8 ♘xc6 are also hopeless for Black) **8 ♕xd4! ♘xd4 9 ♘f6+ ♔f8 10 ♗h6#**.

30. You probably noticed the similarity to the *Levenfish Trap*, but I hope you didn't just snatch the knight off right away: 8 ♕xg4? ♗xb5 is bad since the b5-bishop was undefended, and 8 ♗xd7+? ♕xd7 defends the knight. **8 e6!** shatters Black's coordination. 8...♗xb5 9 exf7+ ♔xf7 10 ♕xd8 costs Black his queen, while after 8...fxe6 9 ♗xd7+ and ♕xg4 White wins a piece. Several high-rated players have fallen for this trap – there was even a game in the Slovenian championship.

31. After **12 ♖e5!** the *Queen is Trapped!* **12...g5 13 ♖xg5 ♕h6 14 ♖xd5** is terrible for Black, so in a master-level game, he preferred to resign instead.

32. **10 d5! ♘a5 11 ♘e5** causes a *Collapse on f7 after Castling Queenside*. **11...♖e8 12 b4** *Traps the Knight* on the edge and after **12...e6 13 bxa5 exd5 14 f4** White has an extra piece.

33. After **7...♘xc3! 8 bxc3** (8 ♖xc3 ♗b4 pins the rook) **8...♗a3** we have a *Rook Cornered by Bishops*. **9 ♖b1 ♗xb1 10 ♕xb1** is White's best try, but **10...♗d6 11 cxd5 exd5 12 ♕xb7 ♘e7** doesn't give him enough play for the lost exchange.

34. With **9...dxc3!** Black understands that White will be *Winning the Queen at Too High a Cost*. After **10 ♗xh7+ ♔xh7 11 ♖xd8 cxb2+ 12 ♔xb2 ♖xd8 13 ♘f3 ♘c6** Black has rook, bishop and knight for queen and two pawns, and an easy attack against the white king. White's days are numbered.

35. The *Standard Sacrifice* **12 ♘d5!** is good. White immediately regains the piece with a huge advantage. **12...exd5** (12...♕b7 13 ♘xc6 ♕xc6?? 14 ♘xe7+ wins the queen) **13 cxd5** followed by taking on c6 leaves White a pawn up with a dominant position.

36. The *Queen is Trapped in the Corner*: **8 axb4! ♕xa1 9 ♘xd4** and ♘b3 will win the black queen.

37. The undefended bishop on b7 and the trappable rook on a8 make **8 ♘xf7!** a clear win. **8...♔xf7** (8...♕b6 9 ♘xh8 leaves Black a rook down) **9 dxe6+** (a *Rampant Pawn*) **9...♔xe6 10 ♗xb7** is hopeless for Black.

38. 8...♗xb2?? is a blunder due to 9 ♗xb2 ♖xb2 10 ♕d4 forking the black rooks, but **8...♖xb2!** *Steals the Cheese*. **9 ♗xb2 ♗xb2 10 ♘d2 ♗xa1 11 ♕xa1 ♘f6** leaves Black a pawn up. Even though it will not be so easy for him to win the ending, it is clearly a very good outcome of the opening for Black.

39. It's the *IQP Trap*: **14 d5! exd5 15 ♗g5** (threatening 16 ♗xf6 followed by ♕xh7#) **15...g6 16 ♖xe7 ♕xe7 17 ♘xd5** and White makes decisive material gains.

40. By taking the piece White clearly wasn't expecting him to, Black brings about *Death on the h-File*. After **10...hxg5!** the threat of ...♛xh2# means White can't save his knight on c6. **11 e5 dxc6!** (11...♛xc6? 12 exf6 lets White fight on) and Black wins a piece.

41. White needs to play **10 g4!** before he can use the *Pin on the e-File* to *Win a Pawn*. It's often risky to push pawns like this in front of our king, but here it wins a good central pawn and White's king remains safe. **10...♗g6 11 ♘xe5! ♗xe5 12 ♖e1 0-0** (or 12...♘c6 13 ♘f3 ♗d7 14 ♘xe5 ♘dxe5 15 d4) **13 ♖xe5** and White is a clear pawn up.

42. 12...♘xe4! is a *Sicilian Unpin*. Black snaps off the well-defended e4-pawn thanks to the loose bishop on g5. After **13 ♗xe7** (or 13 ♘dxe4 ♗xg5) **13...♘xc3 14 bxc3** (14 ♕xe6? fxe6 15 ♗xd8 would avoid losing a pawn were it not for the check 15...♘e2+!) **14...♕xe7** Black is a full pawn up.

43. Black is attacking on the *Long Diagonal* and with a *Rook-Lift*. With **12...♕h4!!** he wins in the same way that White did in Trap 63: **13 ♘f3** (or 13 gxh4 ♖g6+ 14 ♔h1 ♗xf2#) **13...♖g5!! 14 gxh4** (14 ♘xh4 ♘h3#) **14...♘xf3+ 15 ♗xf3** (15 ♔h1 ♖xh4) **15...♖g6+! 16 ♗g2 ♖xg2+ 17 ♔h1 ♖xf2+ 18 ♔g1 ♖xc2**.

44. White *Invades on f7*: **14 ♗xh7+!** (14 ♗xf6 ♗xf6 15 ♗xh7+ ♔f8 is far less clear) **14...♔xh7 15 ♗xf6 ♗xf6 16 ♕h5+ ♔g8 17 ♕xf7+ ♔h7 18 ♘xd7** and White regains his piece, keeping a couple of extra pawns (he can also play for mate with 18 ♖d3!).

45. 15 ♘xd2?? loses the rook on a1, so White *Castles the Intruder Away*: **15 0-0-0!**.

Now Black can do no better than exchange his knight, and White's attack and material plus will carry the day. **15...♘xb3+ 16 axb3 ♘c6** (16...♕a1+ 17 ♔d2 ♕d4+ 18 ♗d3 and the checks soon run out) **17 ♕xh7!** and following ♗c4 White should win comfortably.

46. White *Crashes Through on f7 and e6*: **8 ♘xf7! ♔xf7 9 dxe6+**. The point is that the d7-bishop is pinned, so Black must take with the king or else allow 10 exd7 and be a pawn down. After **9...♔xe6** the king will never make it to safety. **10 ♗c4+ ♔e7 11 ♕e2+ ♔d6 12 0-0!** gives White a winning attack, with ♖d1+, ♗f4+ and ♘a3 in the pipeline.

47. 14 ♗g6!! is a *Horrible Discovery*! White threatens the black queen and mate on f7. **14...♘e2+** (14...♘e5 15 ♗xf7+! deflects the knight, and 15...♘xf7 16 ♖xd4 gives White a queen for two uncoordinated pieces) **15 ♕xe2!** (15 ♔h1?? hxg6 16 ♖xd4 ♘xd4 gives Black *Too Much for the Queen*). Now there is the threat of ♕xe6+, and after **15...♕e5, 16 ♗xf7+! ♔xf7 17 ♖xd7+!** strips away the queen's defender.

48. This position is from analysis of a game between Karpov and Miles, which was a legendary victory for the Englishman. But here White has an *Overwhelming Development* advantage, and wins by piling in: **13 ♘e5!!**. Black is mated if he takes either piece, and mate in two with 14 ♕h5+ is threatened. For instance, 13...fxg5? 14 ♕h5+ ♔f8 15 ♕f7# or 13...fxe5? 14 ♕h5+ ♔f8 15 ♗h6+ ♔g8 16 ♕g4+, etc. 13...0-0 14 ♗h6 gives White a devastating attack, with 15 ♕g4+ threatened. The 'best' defence, 13...h5 14 ♘g6, only allows Black to limp on the exchange down.

Further Improvement

Congratulations – you have reached the end of the book. What is next?

To make sure the ideas have stuck in your mind, briefly go through the book again. On each page, look at the diagrams first. Do you remember the key ideas? Can you work out what's going on? Can you think of similar positions where the same idea works or doesn't work?

Maybe take a look at each position with a computer engine running. If you are reading this book on Chess Studio, you'll be able to turn it on by pressing the engine button. This will help you see how an obvious defence is defeated. Or why other tempting-looking moves don't work. Using computers as a training partner (rather than as an opponent) should become a major part of your work on chess and is how many young players have become strong players at an early age.

Take a look at some grandmaster games, either from a book or by watching them live online. Think about the opening principles the players are following (or ignoring!) and the tactical ideas that crop up. The most important thing, though, is to play lots of games of your own. Analyse them afterwards and learn every lesson you can.

Useful Work:

Understand and remember the traps – *Good!*
Learn the patterns behind the traps – *Better!*
Solve the exercises – *Even better!*
Practise with a friend to use the patterns and traps – *Better still!*
Play competitive games and learn how to make good decisions – *Best of all!*

WINNING THE QUEEN, LOSING THE KING

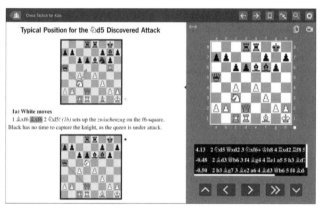